Embracing Defiance:

Helping Your Child Express Their Unique Voice while Keeping Your Sanity

Beth Halbert, PsyD

The biological, psychological, and neurological changes during the transition from childhood to adulthood can be a precarious time. The "Terrible Twos" pale by comparison. Dr. Beth Halbert's advice in her book, *Embracing Defiance*, gives us not just theory, but practical applications and solutions to cope successfully with this transitional stage of development. It serves as a guide to navigate the sometimes stormy, complicated seas of the teenage. Her voice is unique and will help us to remain calm, compassionate, and sane no matter where we are on life's path or stage of growth. We all benefit.

Barbara Findeisen, MA
Founder and Director Star Foundation

All parents should be assigned this book the day their baby is born. *Embracing Defiance* gives you the tools and support you need to make it through all the joys—and challenges— of childrearing with your sanity intact! I can't underscore the benefits of this book, nor can I say enough about the confidence I've gained as I enter the next phase with my own kids.

Alicia Coleman
Mom & Care Peer Group Facilitator Mentor

Embracing Defiance: *Helping Your Child Express Their Unique Voice while Keeping Your Sanity*

Beth Halbert, PsyD

ISBN 978-1-937445-05-8

Library of Congress Control Number: 2011936500

Published by Bush Street Press
237 Kearny Street, #174
San Francisco, CA 94108
415-413-0785
Printed in the United States of America

Dedication

This book is dedicated to my business and life partner, Dora Wallace. Without Dora, this book would not be written. Thank you to my Inner Family: Little B for her vulnerability and courage, Super B for her hard work and dedication, Bubblin' B for her passion and UNIQUE VOICE, and Dr. B for her wisdom and unconditional love.

TABLE OF CONTENTS

Introduction

About the Author

I am Beth Halbert, a.k.a. Dr. Beth, a Licensed Clinical Psychologist and "America's Teenologist," as described by Mom's The Word Radio and various Bay Area Moms Groups. I use the term *Teenology* to describe the study and process of embracing your defiance and awakening to your authentic, powerful, passionate voice. Helping families come together to grow and prepare for the teen years is my passion. It is an honor and a gift to be able to assist teens and young adults from all walks of life launch into adulthood as fully empowered and impassioned human beings.

In my private practice, I have encountered many adults with stifled teen developmental years who feel repressed and powerless. Though time has progressed for these adults, the emotional and sometimes psychological challenges of the "teen years" are still present. The impact this can have on their lives can be detrimental not only to themselves but also to their partners, bosses, co-workers, children, and other loved ones if not addressed.

As I have mentioned, this teen energy is not specific only to teenagers. It can be found in most, if not all, human beings. It is my belief that this teen energy begins as an ember from birth and is expressed non-verbally through the physical body. In toddlers, the teen energy sparks into a flame as verbal communication is learned and expression is unadulterated and emotionally-charged. Around seven years of age, the teen energy tends to implode and the opposite polarity is experienced as we attempt to master being perfect and responsible adults. At the end of the twelfth year, the energy reverses again and gradually builds into a raging bonfire as the teen years begin. By this time, your child may be feeling like all of life has been experienced and their acquisition of knowledge vast. This is the process of individuating as they discover their specific style, their authentic self, their unique voice. The changes you will witness in your child's personality will be enough for you to question your own sanity. I assure you, it's pretty normal. It is this evolution of becoming a fully empowered Teen and the energy associated with it that fuels my work and has led to the creation of this book.

Embracing Defiance: Helping Your Child Express Their Unique Voice while Keeping Your Sanity prepares you and your child for the teen years. As a Clinical Psychologist, I see children and teens every day as they discover and learn to respectfully express their authentic, passionate, *individuated* voices. I also see what happens when teens *don't* find their authentic voices. The longer a person waits to find his or her voice, the more intense the individuation process feels, causing more stress on relationships with others.

Some people never learn how to embrace their own defiance and never find their own powerful voices. By resisting defiance, avoiding conflict, and avoiding speaking your truth, you actually become stuck in your rebellious teen years, and remain so into adulthood. It is through embracing defiance and finding their authentic voices that children enjoy healthy, fun development through the teen years and the rest of their life.

Officially, I am a licensed child, teen, and family psychologist with a big vision and a huge, compassionate heart. Aside from my private practice, I offer parenting workshops and teleconferences through Dr. Beth's Compassionate Parenting Programs. My true passion and purpose is to work with parents and teens/children to create healthy, playful, loving relationships. By helping emotionally healthy parents rear emotionally healthy teens and children, I will create a more playful, peaceful, and joyful world.

Why I Wrote This Book

Most people correlate defiant behavior with teen behavior: what do you think of when you hear someone say a person is "acting just like a teenager?" I've heard many parents say "I have a two-year-old going on her teens," or "I'm dreading when my kid reaches the teen years."

I am writing this book because I have a passion for teens and their intense, powerful energy. I think teens have gotten a really bad rap in society. I have been told by many children that they are scared to death to grow up and become a teenager. This fear will become perfectly clear as we look into this topic a bit further. Almost every adult I've had in my clinical work, workshops, and teleconferences has told me they are petrified to have their children grow into the teen years; they're also scared about just having to interact with teens, as well. It makes for a challenging social climate and cultural environment when society as a whole scapegoats the teens as an entire group.

Many teens don't want to become adults for many "good" reasons. When I ask teens to describe adulthood, their parents, their future adulthood possibilities, they talk about being stressed out, overworked, underpaid, in debt, exhausted, underappreciated, uninspired...I could go on and on.

I wonder where they got these crazy ideas.

One of the reasons that I'm writing this book is because I want to make visible an unconscious invisible prejudice that I have seen impact every race, every socioeconomic group, and every culture in our country. There is another story to tell. There is a silent voice that will soon become the majority and powerfully impact all of our futures—that silent voice is the next generation, our current teens.

I love teen passion, I love teen possibility, I love their leadership, I love their endless energy, I love their idealistic dreams, I love their authentic voices, and I love what they have to bring to the world. Ready or not, they are our next world leaders, so I want to give parents tools to ease their own fears as their children become teens. I want to give the teens a new way to speak, so that they have a way to manage their powerful, intimidating voices. And, at the same time, I want to give teens the tools so they won't be afraid as they become consciously empowered, fully functioning adults.

Without embracing defiance, encouraging defiance, and yes, even *celebrating* defiance, the teen years will continue to be feared, abhorred, and stunted, and those teens will unconsciously re-enact this defiance through adulthood, internally and externally.

How to Use This Book

This book is meant for anyone wanting to understand defiant behavior in oneself and in others. You will be given tools to better understand how your behavior can incite defiance in another, and how your responses and reactions can escalate problematic behavior, or alternatively, minimize and calm a challenging situation. As a parent, you can use this book to look at your own behavior and learn how and why you might be shooting yourself in the proverbial foot. You can also look at how defiance shows up with your children, your spouse, your friends, your work environment (especially in your employees if you are in a leadership position), and most important, how defiance shows up within your own behavior when you feel like you are at war with yourself.

This book is applicable to parents with children of *all* ages. How you might know if this book is right for you:

- If you are challenged and frustrated by others telling you NO, ignoring you, or not cooperating with your intended agenda. (This includes your spouse!)

- If you have a difficult time setting and sticking to your boundaries. (If you are invested in keeping the peace and intend to have happiness around you as much as feasibly possible, this might be you!)

- If you find that you consistently set plans and goals for yourself only to constantly let yourself down and infuriate yourself with your lack of follow-through; if you feel you are not meeting your full potential.

- If you find that you are having difficulty keeping your sanity with your child's defiant behavior.

- If you fear your child growing into the teen years and are thinking "if we continue on this path, I'm not sure how I will handle my child".

- If you fear arguments and conflict and do anything and everything to keep the peace, including selling yourself short and not getting your needs met.

This book is applicable to teens and young adults of *all* ages, as well. How you might know if this is right for you:

- If you are a teen and you have no idea why you keep shooting yourself in the foot.

- If you are a young adult who wants to leave your parents' home, and you feel like you are trapped or stuck in a bad situation and you don't know how to get yourself out.

- If you are a child who fears growing into the teenage years and would like to set yourself up for a smooth transition from childhood into personal empowerment and responsibility.

- If you are a teen who is confused about why one moment you feel like you are still a very young child and the next you have no idea why you still have to follow your parents' rigid rules and unreasonable expectations for your life.

- If you are a teen who is ready to own the conscious creation, responsibility, and empowerment of your own destiny, despite what your parents have done, or are not doing.

- If you want to better understand and live into healthy adult choices, 100% empowerment, mature adult development, and passionate, authentic self-expression.

This book is not meant as a replacement for legal, medical, or clinical psychological help. This book is not meant as a prescription for specific legal, ethical, or psychological issues with teens. If you are dealing with a crisis, emergency situation, or difficult defiance issue that feels out of control or unmanageable, get help from a qualified professional. Call 911, your family pediatrician, therapist, or other caregiver. For less emergent issues, refer to the resource section at www.drbeth.com/embracingdefiance for additional tools and resources.

Defiance 101

I was working with a child in my office, and I made a guess at what might be underneath his behavior and acting out. He felt so understood, seen, gotten, that when his parents joined us in the session, he asked me to explain what and why he did what he did. He said, "You know me better than I know myself." Many times our unconscious thoughts get acted out when we are not seeing or understanding these thoughts or stories we have about ourselves, and others.

So, you may be thinking *it is one thing to push or ask for what you need—and another thing entirely to be outright rude, hurtful, tacky, aggressive, attacking*.

What if I told you again, *Congratulations!* Your child is moving to the next developmental stage of growth and exploration.

So what does it mean when they say, "Your hair looks funny. Why are you wearing that outfit? What's wrong with you? You embarrass me! What were you thinking?"

What if the child is doing this because she is looking for her expert, YOU, her hero, and her ideal God figure, to tell her what the answer is? She is watching to see what you would do in such a situation. Children go through this every day with their peers, with their inner teen voices in their heads, with everyone around them. They don't know how to respond and feel barraged with change, criticism, and confusion. So they throw some of these tests at you, the people who are up on this huge pedestal, so they can see how *you* would handle some of their life challenges. I would even go so far as to say if they are saying it to you, it is really something that they think or fear to be true *about themselves*.

The key to this stage is not to take it personally, not to go down with the punch, not to go into your young-defensive state and punch back. (More on this in a bit.)

The type of reaction we want to effect is a two-step process.

The first step is to get curious about what statements penetrate your confident, compassionate, loving exterior. For example, if your child called you a pink polka-dotted elephant, would you care? Would you believe her? Would you go into your room, crying your eyes out? Would you ground him for life? Would you need a support group to challenge and question the validity of the statement? Of course not! My question is *why not?*

What if your child said you were a terrible mother or father? What if your child said you looked fat or outdated? What if they challenged your parenting boundary as over-controlling and unyielding?

Would you believe any one of these statements to be true? Children don't know or believe this judgment as a fact any more than if they had called you a pink polka-dotted elephant!

So if you believe the statement, or feel wounded by it, that is only because there is some part of you that believes there is actually some truth to, and feels bad-and-wrong about, the judgment.

If a severely drunken homeless person screamed the same statements to you while walking by on the street, would the words sting? Would you believe it as your truth? Why do we choose to give our children power over our emotional state?

My challenge to you is to *take your power back*.

If there is something that stings, go within and see if it is something you want to address. If you are told you are the meanest, strictest, most out-of-date parents on the block, do some research and see if that is actually true. Call a child and family psychologist, interview teachers, other parents of children your child's age, and ultimately go within and see if your decision resonates with your inner, wise self.

The second step is to give your child feedback and an authentic reaction to his way of being with you. One way you can do this is to become an explorer with your child and get curious about the new behavior, the new criticism, the new way your child is looking at you and the world. You can even say,

Wow, how interesting. You are really noticing a lot of negative things about my life, my body, intensely taking my inventory. I wonder what that is about? Because truth be told, I actually love this outfit, my hairdo, and my way of being in public. So by expressing these extremely hurtful negative assessments of me, I know this is less about me and how I show up in life, and more about how you are feeling, what's going on inside of you, and I'm wondering if you are needing something from me.

What you are doing is letting the child know that words have the possibility of stinging, *without allowing them to sting*.

If your child went out into the world and said the exact same statements to her friends, family, or future employers, you know that they would lose relationships and potentially their jobs. So the key is to let your child know how the statement feels to you and how it initially impacts you, without taking the comments as your truth unless you *choose* to own it as your truth. (If so, you can wear the assessment with a badge of honor and be proud of your loser, 80s style, your outdated expressions, or whatever else is being noticed by your child. If you choose to create a new you, do it for you, not for your child.)

It is just as important not to forcefully or punitively stop the behavior. The behavior is informative and very telling as to what is going on within your child's inner world. If your child is telling you that you are an idiot, it may very well be because he is feeling stupid, scared, insecure, and uncertain of whom he is at this time of his life, unsure of what to think, and is questioning what he knows as his truth.

After first addressing your own insecurities and questions, and second allowing your child to notice with you the hurtful, negative behavior, the next phase is to get your child to participate and get curious with you about what the judgments, defiant behavior, and hurtful reactions may actually be about.

How might these hurtful communications be serving you and your child? There will be more information to help unravel this gift later in this book, and on my website, www.drbeth.com/embracingdefiance.

1. What is Teenology?

Teenology is the study of:

- the teen years,
- the stages of teen development,
- the study of defiance by finding and expressing your authentic compassionate voice
- the parenting and mentoring to prepare for the teen years, and
- the understanding of the internal teen character and energy.

Teenology is an understanding of the aspects of coming into the teen years, feelings while "stuck" in the teen years, and the method to move forward and through the teen years for both parents and teens.

Teenology is the understanding of society's negative story of teen character logical states versus a brand new paradigm of new world leaders utilizing the passion and authentic voice of teen energy.

Teenology is the study of teen energy—in people of all ages! I'll introduce you to toddler teens, preteens, teens, and ready-to-launch adult teens.

Teenology is also the study of parents dealing with children embracing their teen energy, as well as their current, actual teenager.

And, finally, *Teenology* is the study of a brand-new concept that I call "The Inner Teenager."

I will walk you through all the developmental stages, what is natural, normal, and healthy, and we will explore and debunk some of the misconceptions that people have about teens and healthy teen development.

Why is Teenology Important to Society?

What stories does society have about teens? If teens live into how we see them, we are going to have one hellacious world! So if we see teens as bad mamma-jammas, thugs, thieves, drug addicts, what else—what are the odds they will mature into anything else?

What is your story or fear your child will live into when he reaches the teen years?

Many parents find these fears intimidating or scary. Parents may feel out of control and fear their children are at high-risk. I did a workshop/radio show with a group of twenty-five inner-city teens. They were bused in from a San Francisco project area into one of the wealthiest school districts in Marin County, Northern California. They came in with their hats on sideways, their chains dangling, and their pants down along their hips. The typical teen bad-ass attitude practically hissed off of them as I walked in the room. If looks could kill, I would be dead.

I asked them: "What does society think about you? About teenagers?" As I captured their responses on my flip chart, they easily filled up a couple of pages of all of these horrible, horrible things that society says about teens.

At the end of their highly energized, shock-and-awe rant, I said after a dramatic pause: "I don't buy it!" You could have cut the room with a knife. Every gaze in the room pierced a hole through me as they tried to figure out my angle.

But it wasn't hostility I saw on their faces—it was disbelief! *I can't believe she really sees me. Someone finally sees that I don't want to be a bad person, I don't want to be a bad teen.*

With that, the attitude in the room just...changed! It was like the hats were automatically straightened, the baggy pants came into a more comfortable position, the kids were sitting up in their chairs, hanging on to my next words for the following two hours. I did not think they were ever going to stop dancing and leave after the workshop was over. They just hung out and loved to be around the possibility that someone actually saw their beauty and totally believed in them—even though they had done their best to present all evidence and past behavior to the contrary.

How do Teens Impact Society?

Based on data from the National Center for Education Statistics and the U.S. Department of Education, right now:

- 11% of teens drop out of school

- 16,964 are suspended from school

- 4,356 are arrested

- About a third of all victims of violent crime (physical assault, sexual assault/rape, physical abuse, robbery, etc.) are ages 12 to 19, and almost half of all victims of violence were under age 25.

- Suicide is the third highest cause of death among teenagers. Teenagers attempt suicide every minute, and one succeeds every two hours.

- Every 7 minutes, a student in the United States is bullied; every day, 160,000 American students miss school because of bullying.

- 227 children and adults have been killed in our schools since the Columbine incident in 1999.

And if we continue to believe the statistics, the stories, the inevitable outcomes, and the thoughts the children are internalizing, then our children and teens have no other unconscious choice but to live into these current statistics. So, if we can change the story, then we can change the possibility for teens, and ultimately we can change the outcome for our future world leaders.

As if it were not enough to deal with societal stories of their inevitable fates, teens have daily pressures that rival those of adults. Many adults would never trade their current stresses for their child's daily mental barrage, but even if you remember how difficult it was when you were a teen, rest assured that today's teens have it even harder.

Why is Teenology Important to Younger Children?

So, let me give you a left-handed, or roundabout, answer to this question by telling you a story.

A nine-year-old boy attended one of my workshops, "Dealing Deftly with Defiance," with his parents. It's really written for parents, but this child came along for the ride.

At the end of the workshop, I asked him questions.

"What do you think? What did you learn?"

"My life will never be the same again," was his instant reply.

I laughed and said, "Yeah, but what did you *think*?"

"No. Really. My life will never be the same again." And he said this over and over again, about five times!

"But how will your life never be the same?"

"I finally know that I don't have to be a bad teenager. It's my choice."

"Wow!" I said. "How did you get that out of the workshop?"

And this amazing nine year old said, "Just because my parents smoke, doesn't mean I have to smoke."

And the most interesting thing behind this scene is that his parents did not even smoke!

In the workshop, I had used the smoking story for the parents to make the point that when you walk the talk, your kids follow your footsteps. This boy got that concept, and in his little nine-year-old mind got in his own challenging power—I call this defiance. Effectively, he was saying *Oh no, I won't! I do have a choice and I don't have to live into my parents' choices and life experiences.*

So for children, Teenology is giving them a conscious choice to make life choices different than those of their parents and of society's beliefs about them. It is giving them a choice to see that they are ultimately the creator and owner of their own actions, behaviors, results, and futures.

I have another example of child insight and personal choice. During another parenting workshop, there was a young girl, eleven or twelve years old. I watched how carefully she sought her mother's approval and acknowledgement as she participated in the workshop. So I decided to name the proverbial pink elephant in the room. I asked: "Do you think your mom is ready for you to grow up and become a teenager?" As serious as she could be, she said, "No, not quite." Then I asked if *she* was ready. She smiled and looked at her mother to see if *her mother* was okay with her answer. The more we talked, this girl was able to verbalize both her fears of growing into the teen years, as well as her fear of losing her mother when she became a fully-functioning teenager.

And so we understood why she was trying to stay young, acting very young for her age, because she didn't want to become one of those "bad" teens that would no longer get to snuggle into mommy's arms and stay close to her mom for the rest of her life. So I worked with both of them to figure out a way that they could both have a life where they stayed emotionally connected while, at the same time the young child had an option to *individuate*—have different beliefs and thoughts—and thus, eventually, become a separate person and emotionally de-cord from her mother. With this support and preparation, this girl has a strong base for the challenges to come, as well as the opportunity to grow up into becoming a fully-functioning empowered adult. Most important, she had a new possibility that she could enjoy living and growing into her teenage years, as well as one day looking forward to becoming an adult. What an innovative concept!!!

Do You Remember Being a Child? How About Being a Teen?

Today's societal pressures cause children and teens to face multiple challenges each day. Take a moment to remember what it was like when you were a teenager.

Stress of getting up and out the door on time. Research shows that due to changing body-clock rhythms, it is actually more difficult for teens to get up early in the a.m. Their body rhythms are more attuned to staying up late and getting up late. Some school systems are starting the younger grades earlier and letting the high schools start last, because this results in better attendance, fewer tardies, and higher test scores.

Stress of keeping up with school. In school, teens study a wide range of topics in which they have very little personal interest. They see very little purpose in learning, other than to be controlled and jump through an adult's willy-nilly school action plan. Teenagers didn't vote on school testing! And they hate feeling responsible or blamed for teachers and schools losing income and funding.

Stress of peer pressure. Even if they say they don't, most teens want to fit in. They bear the stress of trying to look cool, not just to fit in, but also so they don't become the next physical or emotional scapegoat, with their name written on the bathroom walls. Also, it's stressful to stay "in the know" and keep up with all the Facebook, e-mail, texting, and social media matters, not to mention the stresses associated with finding out what their peers think of them. Teens have tremendous peer pressure to belong, fit in, not stick out too much. At the same time, there is pressure and competition to be different, for each teen to find and express his or her authentic, unique voice.

Stress from parents and family. Teens are under pressure to please their parents and keep them happy, and also to keep themselves from losing privileges such as computer time, driving, etc. It's a particularly tough conundrum: teens' natural inclination at this stage of development is to desire individuation. They do this by meticulous observation to find what's different and by critically judging their parents. Try being critical and judging while at the same time pleasing another...fuhgeddaboutit!

There may also be the pressure of a single-parent or two-home living situation, and financial pressures, such as a part-time job. Teenagers may also experience parental physical or emotional abuse.

Stress from alcohol or drug issues. Teens may not be emotionally able to handle the peer pressure associated with alcohol and drug use: *everyone is doing it; I'll die if I experiment; I'll become an addict; my parents will kill me; I will be arrested*; or for those with the strength to decline: *I will be seen as a loser and a geek.* Underneath the obvious pressures, teens are dealing with such huge emotions, conflicted beliefs, and challenging situations, that they might enjoy the numbing and medicating effects of an inebriated quick fix.

Stress from sexual situations. At earlier and earlier ages, teens may be confronted with sex and sexual situations via television, computer, peers, etc. In addition to these external stimuli, teens are having sexual awakenings and sensations, and may begin sexual activity at a young age. Whether sexually active or not, teens may experience date violence or stalking, which can happen to both boys and girls.

Stress from bullying. Bullying happens across all socioeconomic and geographic boundaries. Teens may be bullied by classmates, friends, siblings, and in rare cases, teachers or parents. Bullying in cyberspace can be even more devastating, as the bullying may be broadcast to a much wider audience, whether or not the victim is even aware it is happening, and once discovered, the victim has very little recourse.

Stress from learning disorders. Teens who have learning or other disorders, such as attention-deficit, AD/HD, sensory integration issues, illnesses, or other physiological health challenges, may face additional stress. While support at school or through private therapies (speech/language or occupational therapy, for example) may help the teen with schoolwork or physical challenges, the simple fact of needing the support may be cause for unwanted attention from peers.

Stress from growing up. Teens struggle with self-esteem: who am I, anyway? They deal with hormonal rages, extreme moods (highs and lows), and body changes, both expected and unexpected.

Why is Teenology Important to Teens?

Of all questions, this is probably one of the most important. *Teens are to become our next world leaders*. This is where our future is heading. If we don't change stories, the vision, and the possibilities for our teens right now, our world will be potentially destroyed. That may be a bit over the top. It may sound like an off-the-wall statement, but I see teens and their struggles. I work with teens every single day, and many are feeling helpless, hopeless, and devastated as they move into adulthood. I also have many parents tell me they are having a difficult time getting their young-adult children out of the house.

Both frustrated parents and scared-to-death teens are feeling challenged to move on to the next natural, healthy stage of development: *individuation.*

Individuation is the psychological process of moving from the compliant, "easy" childhood years to the vocal, opinionated teen years. Individuation is the child's often-jarring, threatening realization that she does not share her parents' identity, and may actually have different ideas, wants, beliefs, life choices, and make entirely different decisions from her parents. When this concept first becomes a reality for a child, it is discombobulating at best. If I'm not my parent, then who am I? If I'm not my parent, life can certainly feel unsafe, unknown, and filled with overwhelming uncertainty, to say nothing yet of the parent's reaction.

And it's not just disruptive for the teenager: the parents don't know how their teen is going to handle the burdens of the world any more than the teen does! And on top of that, the parent has a significant investment, or attachment, to how the teen "turns out."

So with all this uncertainty as teens try to navigate the choice of staying in compliance versus diving off a cliff into the unknown, it is *essential* that teens understand their natural, age-appropriate reactions. What's happening to them is normal. They are not crazy for wanting to take their parents down and get the heck out of the house, then ten minutes later, wanting to go back into their proverbial happy-childhood womb, flop down on the couch, and ask them for some money.

Individuation is essential for teens to become empowered, accountable, responsible adults. I call the teenage years the ready-to-launch stage. If individuation is not supported, teens may fail to launch, because neither the parents nor the teens have the confidence or the tools to move developmentally forward in life.

When I give the teens a chance, every time, 100% of the time, they are able to tap into their future wise self and tell me the answer for our society. If we will listen to the teens, they have the answers, for themselves and for us.

What is the "Bad Teen" Rap?

We talk about bad teen rap, and I just can't say enough about this story or concept...if we have a story that teens are negative, we get to be right. They will *live into* that negative story.

I worked with a teen who was told when he was four or five years old, in pre-school or kindergarten, that he would never learn how to read. I'm not sure if a teacher really made such an assessment and said it out loud to the child at such a young age. I was not there, and by the time I met this teen years later, I was, of course, getting the story second-hand. I tend to believe in people and assume the teacher was doing the best he could at the time. Nevertheless, this is what the child heard and understood, and he believed it as the "gospel truth." He would never learn how to read: that was just a God-given fact.

He lived right into that declaration, that story, that belief.

As of the time he was in 7th grade, he was unable to read at all. He was in a learning disability classroom, one for slow learners. His parents and teachers were at their wits' end. No one could figure out why he was unable to read. I asked him why he thought he was unable to read. He told me his story, that his teacher in pre-school or kindergarten told him he would never be able to read, and he said, "I guess he is right. I've tried and tried and I'm not able to learn the reading concepts."

I talked to him about a concept I call *Own Your Story* and took him through a process that transformed his young life. (See www.drbeth.com/embracingdefiance for a complimentary excerpt of the course.) During this process, he learned the concept that someone else's belief or story *does not make it your truth*. He got this so deep within his mind that he became totally vigilant to break the story and make his teacher wrong. He actually grasped the concept and turned it totally around. By his senior year in high school, he had become salutatorian, the second-highest honor in his high school. He transformed and overcame the story; he overcame the declared belief, and created his own true story.

So what we tell our children, whether it's positive or negative, we get to be right. This is where a new, radical concept needs to be introduced. Just because an adult believes something to be true *does not necessarily make it true for the child*. The adult may have a limiting belief of his own. There may be generations of stories holding adults and children hostage to life's limitless possibilities.

If a child believes everything that parents, teachers, and adults say as his truth, we would have very few changes in conscious evolution. For example, based on the adult's life experiences and past stories, children would have been told it is not possible to fly, it is not possible to create a vaccine that prevents chicken pox, it is not possible to walk on the moon, etc. If all children took the status quo as the status quo, we would not have the creations that we currently have the luxury to enjoy in our lives.

Defying adult stories and other limiting belief systems could be the most positive saving grace for the next generation.

What is Positive About Defiance?

Obviously, this sounds like an oxymoron. It's upside-down thinking in the traditional world. Any time I tell parents, "Congratulations, your child is defiant," they look like they want to defiantly slap me upside the head. The truth is, if your child cannot tell you *no*, they also cannot tell the drug dealer *no*, they cannot tell their boyfriend *no*, they cannot tell their over-working hard boss in society *no*. They can't say yes to life, to conscious choice, without knowing how to and having the freedom to say no and speak their truth.

The best place to practice and learn such a scary, unfamiliar, uncomfortable process as *no* is to practice on the person or people with whom your child feels most comfortable.

This is the person they know will always love them, the person they most admire and respect to see how *they* say no, and how they speak their truth when their boundaries are crossed. When children learn how to speak up to you, then they will have the opportunity to believe it is even possible to stand up and speak their truth with anyone outside the family.

So when I say congratulations, I'm saying your child feels safe enough to practice one of the hardest concepts in the world. Standing in their authentic truth, disagreeing with the person they most love and admire, and standing in their power when it goes against every teaching bone in their fiber—because ultimately, almost all kids want to please their parents. I would say *all kids*, but that might cause a defiant reaction in you, the reader. But for the record, I have never seen a child that did not wish to please their parent—the challenging cases have just never found a way to win.

So when they push for an extra hour, one more time, more money, more of anything from you, that feels like you are being pushed and pushed and pushed. It is because you *are* being pushed! Make no mistake, they are pushing. This is part of the trial-and-error learning process.

What happens when I push? What happens when I ask for more? What happens when I have needs that are different than others? Do I have a right to ask? Does the other person have a right to say no? How will they say no and protect themselves when they are pushed and pushed?

If your child is in defiance, pushing, teenage-outrageous space, it is because you have created an environment that is safe enough to move to the next level of mature development.

It is time for them to come out of the compliant childish stage and into the next stage of exploring, to find their voice, and you just happen to be the safest training ground around. Congratulations!!!

Compliance vs. Defiance

You may say, "My child never experienced compliant childish stage. I never had that luxury." Or you may be one of the lucky parents who looks around and wonders why all the other children jump when anyone tells them to jump. Why do all the other children sit when they are told to sit, stay in line, observe the rules, while your child is running all over the place, has something to say about everything, cries and screams when everyone else is quiet as a mouse? *Well it is obvious*, you have told yourself over and over again: you must have done something terribly wrong to destroy the compliant gene in your child. You were not strict enough. You were too strict. You worked too many hours. You were too loving and giving when they were an infant, or you may say it actually started the day they were born. So in that case, you may say you drank or ate something you should not have eaten while you were pregnant. Or you may be telling yourself it was the rock concert or fight I had with my husband or parents. The stories are absolutely endless. I have heard thousands and thousands of stories trying to convince me that the parent was responsible for the child's unruly, obnoxious, annoying, disgusting, embarrassing behavior.

How does it make you feel to believe you have bad genes? That you blew it when they were in the womb? Or that you totally screwed up in the formative years; you didn't feed yourself or your child the right nutrition? Or you said or didn't say the right thing at the right time? Or married the wrong person, or live in the wrong neighborhood?

What is your story about why your child misbehaves, and how does it make you feel to believe the story?

So what if I told you that however your child is behaving is *absolutely perfect and divine?* Our job is to figure out why they are acting the way they are acting—to figure out why they say what they are saying, but not to take it as the truth of what they believe about you.

Steve's mom, Georgia, told me how she'd been having trouble getting him up to go to school on time. She told him if he didn't go to school, he wouldn't get to play his Xbox on the weekends— his best-favorite reward. In fact, Steve often hid the Xbox remotes so Georgia wouldn't be able to take them away! This time, though Georgia one-upped Steve and took the Xbox cables instead. Not to be outmaneuvered, Steve sneaked downstairs and swiped Georgia's cell phone, which was a requirement of her job! Even though Georgia and Steve were normally relaxed with each other and had a history of playful one-upmanship, for Georgia, this was way over the line. It took some serious negotiation, but Georgia got her phone back, Steve got his Xbox cables back, and they made it to work—and school!—on time. Georgia laughingly said she had to do her yoga deep-breathing just to get through it that morning!

Read and share defiant stories at
www.drbeth.com/embracingdefiance

They may not even understand, themselves, why they are doing what they are doing. The behavior is a cover for some unconscious feeling, thought, desire, or need. If we stomp out the behavior before we understand the reason for the acting out, we might miss the most important message our child has to say. (If your child were hurt, bleeding, would you give her a time-out? Threaten her? Take away her car keys? No! You would figure out how to stop the bleeding and comfort her!)

First, understand that even if you can't see the physical reason, *there is always an emotional reason for acting out.* There is an emotional bleeding and wound that we need to find and heal.

The child is trying to get some help in meeting a need, sharing a message, being seen. Our job as parents is to *get curious*, really curious, when any irrational, illogical, off-the-wall behavior is happening. Instead of trying to stomp out the undesirable behavior, we need to find the emotional gusher and address the child's unconscious pain or hurt.

A Note on Not Going Down with the Punch

Your child may or may not have the corner on you, on perfect parenting styles, ideal fashion design, or any other assumption or declaration they project onto you. If you are triggered by her words, it is up to you to do some real soul-searching to see if there is any truth in the trigger. If you do find a basis for her words and you don't like it—*own it and change it*.

You decide if you want to create a new story and a new possibility to live into, for both you and your child.

If you go within and determine your child's observations are absolutely not your truth, this is a good time to question your blinders and unconscious actions. You might want to check with someone you trust, someone who can tell you *no* and has nothing to lose if they tell you their truth. Ask the person you trust if they see any truth in whatever triggered you.

One way to find your truth is to look at your wishes, desires, wants, and needs for your children, your partner, your employees, anyone else you are telling what to do, when to do it, and how to do it. See if any of these admonitions for others might actually be prescriptions for your own life. My challenge to you is to look within and define, own, and create your own story, one *you* want to live into.

This may be a difficult lesson for you to embrace for yourself first, but it is an invaluable lesson to model for your child.

What is the Perfect Super-Kid Syndrome?

Sometimes, I say the politically incorrect thing, and I'm about to do it again.

The truth is, when a parent comes to me and says, "Here, fix my defiant, unruly, non-cooperative child," I'm often wondering if there's another child in the family that is cooperative, perfect, and doing everything right. Nine out of ten times, I will hear about this other child becoming "defiant" after the "identified bad child" starts working with me.

Parents will tell me that they have another child and he's doing great. He is making straight A grades, has all the friends, is captain of the football team, head cheerleader, mastered seven different languages, always cleans his room, loves to help me clean the house, does everything I tell him to do, when I tell him to do it, how I tell him to do it, and where and when I tell him to do it. She or he is absolutely perfect!

The teacher tells me this child sits in the back of the classroom like a quiet little angel, or she is very participative and cooperative at the front of the class—"your child never causes me any problems." Parents tell me they always get positive reports from the teachers, everybody loves their child.

Now for the dramatic pause, these are the children that I'm most concerned about not **yet** having their voice. I fear that when that child begins to mature, the parent will not be prepared for the bottled-up energy and unexpressed anger. And it's downright *scary* to have a child with total compliance.

Ask me why? Because I was one of those children. This is the story of my journey and the journey of many of my adult clients. Often, it isn't until a person reaches their 30s and 40s that he begins to have the courage to find his authentic voice, even if only on the inside. And this achievement is well short of speaking up, defying, and causing challenging problems for others!

The way the super-perfect syndrome, if not addressed, can show up later is in drug and alcohol abuse, chronic illness, anorexia, bulimia, shoplifting, workaholism, gambling, depression, and cutting, to name but a few.

In pretty much anything that I can't say out loud or accept as my authentic truth, I end up taking out the pain on myself on the inside. I become conflicted with what I feel and how I want to show up to the world. So I either deny my needs and/or numb my feelings. This way, there is no conflict in how I see myself as the perfect, compliant, nice person, and how I feel on the inside with my "normal outrageous non-pretty human emotions," such as mad, sad, hurt, disgusted, jealous, and on and on.

The defiant child, on the other side of the coin, has exactly the same conflict, wanting to be seen as a good, perfect, lovable child, yet is unable to pull off the charade. The defiant child feels horrible for having all the normal human emotions like mad, sad, hurt, disgusted, jealous, and on and on. Instead of internalizing the uncomfortable feelings, this child's conflict is acted out *externally*. The compliant children act out their feelings *internally or externally, behind your back.*

And so it's absolutely essential that we're able to find another healthy alternative other than hurting ourselves or hurting others.

And to explore these alternatives, sometimes children move back and forth between compliance and defiance.

What are the Alternatives to Defiance or Compliance?

So it's not to say that defiance and compliance aren't alternatives. There is actually a time to be defiant. If somebody tells you, "Have sex with me" and you don't want to have sex, be defiant. If somebody tells you, "Here, smoke this" and you don't want to smoke, don't smoke. If somebody tells you, "The building's on fire, run for your life," and the building is actually on fire, I suggest you comply and run as fast as you can.

If somebody said, "I've got a million dollars for you, would you like to cash this check?" Abso-fricken-lutely cash the check, fast! Right?

And then again, would you like to have your child ask some questions and do some research before they spend the million? Is it legal? Is there a repayment expectation, with exorbitant interest rates? What is the expectation for cashing the check? Did I just give away my first-born?

And there's the rub, so to speak: if I'm doomed to impulsively defy or comply, there is no time to be still and even consider what options might be in my highest good.

So, not to say that defiance and compliance aren't good options, but there are times when you need a third alternative.

That alternative is what I call *Conscious Self-Reliance* on making a *free choice,* or *making a conscious choice.* And the way you find that alternative is to go within, ask, and listen. This option is learning how to live into one's own conscious reliance.

I like to teach by stories so here is another story to make this point. I was asked to be a guest speaker in a high school psychology classroom. During my presentation, I asked one of the teens where he wanted to go to college. He said emphatically, "I want to go to Berkeley!"

I warned him that I was going to do a psychological experiment and temporarily turn into his mom right before his eyes. Of course, I had never met his mom, and I could not actually turn into his mom. I said "Okay are you ready? Poof!

I'm your mom, and not only are you going to go to Berkeley, if you don't go to Berkeley, I will die. It's so important to me that you go to Berkeley that my life depends on you going to Berkeley."

This child screamed, no lie, in front of all his peers: "I'm not going to Berkeley, and you can't make me!"

I said, "Okay, this experiment is way too dangerous, so I will have to end our role-play early to protect your future education."

I said, "I'm really not your mom! I'm no longer your mom!" I continued, "Now who controlled you in that role play?"

He said, "I did!"

I asked, "Really who controlled you? You told me earlier that you wanted to go to Berkeley. Was that not really your truth?"

He looked at me stunned and confused, not knowing how to be in his power in this moment. He was willing to give up the school of his dreams to keep his dignity, personal control, and personal sense of power.

I said, "Actually I controlled you into not going to Berkeley. I could have won a million-dollar bet that you would have changed your mind in order not to be controlled by me, or really by your pretend mom."

"So, what I want you to understand is that by being defiant to me or really, your mom, we are still controlling you." When he got that, you could see the light bulbs going off in his head.

When she was a teen, Angela's mom wanted her to go to a prestigious private high school, one with an entrance exam. During the test, Angela just scribbled circles all over the paper. Mom lost her testing fee, and Angela got to go to her regular high school, after all. No matter what the parent is attached to, it's the child who ultimately has the power to pass or fail a test at her whim.

Read and share your personal teen defiant stories at www.drbeth.com/ embracingdefiance

---

"So let me ask again as your mom being attached to where you go to school, where are you going to college?"

Again, you could see the boy's conflict.

He said, "If she wanted me to go there, I don't know if I could do it."

"I totally get it," I said, and his response is perfectly age-appropriate.

If parents could get this one concept and not be attached to anything the child is already committed to, life would be so much easier for everyone.

A parent being attached to a specific college is the kiss of death for that child to be easily able to make a free choice. A parent wanting, needing, or having their parental success based on their child making good grades creates age-appropriate internalized conflict within their child. What most parents don't know or trust about their child is that most, if not all, children already, naturally, and intuitively want to be successful and accomplished if they believe it is possible, if they are physically able to learn and succeed, and most important, if they don't feel like they are living their lives as a controlled puppet, only to make good grades for your edification. In this last case, it is as if they are selling their soul, or selling their free will, their free choice, to another if they do what you want them to do—even if that choice would have been what they'd choose for themselves.

Let's check out one more of my stories from the high school classroom. I asked, "Would everyone like to experience a decision of total free choice and conscious self-reliance?" They were all up for the challenge. I said to everyone in the classroom, with enthusiasm and boisterous control, "Sit down right now! And I do mean everybody—sit down right now!"

By the way, they were all already sitting.

I shouted, "I mean it, you had better stay seated, or else!" and several of them popped out of their seats defiantly, like, Oh yeah? You and what army are going to *make* me stay in this comfortable, seated position?

I said, "Okay, I have a question for those of you who choose to stand up. Did you want to sit down? Were you comfortable sitting in your chair before I said with force that I wanted you to stay comfortable in that seated position?"

And they said, "Sure, I was comfortable until you tried to control me into sitting there."

I said, "So who controlled you to stand up?" and they said, "You did!"

That's right! So if you really have free choice and conscious self-reliance, it's when your parent says to you "Sit Down!" and you are already sitting down, you are comfortable sitting down, you would choose to stay seated if they had not come into the room or had an opinion of any kind, and you choose to stay seated despite your parent wanting you to be seated.

I asked, "Who really cares if your parents want you to be seated, if you *also* want to be seated?"

They were very confident and felt they had mastered this concept of conscious self-reliance. So I asked them if they'd like to try a harder one. I told them: the same thing is true for your education. I asked "How many here want to graduate?" Every hand, 100% in the room went up, and this happens every time I do this exercise with teens and children of all ages, for that matter.

I said, "Really, then what happens when your parent says 'Do your homework before you play that game!'? You need to do homework to graduate, right?"

They all said "YES!" Someone added, "But I don't want to be controlled! It is none of their business when I do my homework." (I left that discussion on the table for another day.)

Then I said, "So if you all agree you want to graduate, and you all agree you have to do homework to graduate, I'm assuming you all will choose to do your homework every night."

At this point, heads started exploding in the room. "The only way you can have free choice and conscious self-reliance is to make up your mind whether you want to graduate or not. Regardless of the fact that your parents are going to get a huge kick out of you graduating, they might even take all the credit for your accomplishments and get all sentimental and proud and buy you presents, *you* must decide it is okay for your parents to have the delusion that they did your homework, that they had the power, and they are responsible for your accomplishments and your success. You can know in your heart of hearts that you wanted to graduate for *you*, not for anyone else. You can know unequivocally that it was actually *you* that did the homework, you that passed all those tests, and you that made the grades…Not for your parents, not for their joy and edification, but because it was your free choice and your conscious self-reliance and hard work."

Most of the teens understood, agreed, and said, "That's right, I would stay seated if that's what I wanted. I do my homework and study for me, not for my parents."

Interestingly enough, even in such a playful demonstration, you could see and hear the conflict in some of the teens still fighting to resist being controlled. These would be the same children who would choose not to eat for weeks or months if they felt controlled by their parents.

Those of you who have one of these children know exactly what I'm talking about. There is no way to win with a powerfully-minded defiant child. They would rather die than let you win. Then again, you may know this person intimately, during those times when you have shot yourself in the foot to make sure you weren't being controlled by your parents, your spouse, your boss or even to be in the control battle to begin with, over such an important thing like eating that specific vegetable, that night, during that specific allotted time, that you determined to be essentially life and death. I do this same "sit, stand, because I said so" exercise in adult parenting classes, and some of you adults stand when I do the demonstration. You know who you are!! NONE of us like to be controlled.

As a parent, what can you learn from this demonstration? Once your child has determined that you're attached to a particular food choice, that food choice automatically becomes a battle of wills.

Interestingly enough, in the absence of parental input, many children don't even know what they would prefer to begin with. Some children get paralyzed with fear in decision-making if they can't figure out *your* preference.

I tell parents: it is so hard for children to find their power and find their voice because they are trying to please you, or trying not to upset you, or trying not to be controlled. So in matters where physical safety is not a primary concern, why not let your child practice thinking for herself?

Let me give you another example. I took one of my family members shopping at the beginning of the school year. Our task was to find the perfect backpack to carry all his books. Knowing how difficult it can be for me to make decisions and always looking to please others, I had a hidden secondary task, which was to make sure I did not continue the intergenerational patterns. I challenged myself to give no input or clue as to my preference in the matter. We were there for over 30 minutes, with him attempting to read my mind on my preference.

Some children have not been given or have not taken the time to know for themselves whether they want to sit or stand, do homework and learn or fail, play or graduate.

It will help your child so much if you ask them questions to ponder about their own lives. What are their thoughts, what are their feelings, what are their desires, needs, plans, and decisions? You may say *I ask and they won't tell me anything* or *they just say 'I don't know.'*

They only don't know because it is not safe for them to know, or they have not had the chance to practice this muscle of knowing what they think, feel, and desire. What if what they wanted was different than what you wanted them to think or feel? How would you both deal with that catastrophe?

The hardest part is to ask these questions with absolutely no attachments, having no demands, not telling them what to do, what to think, when to do it, how to do it—otherwise, they have to go through the defiance process, back to compliance and back to defiance, and in this process of extremes, figure out what is it they really want to do.

So, the best gift you can give your child is to have no attachments to their thoughts, their feelings, their choices, their behavior, their outcomes, their results, and ultimately, their life. I know I might as well have said jump off a cliff while you are at it. Easier said than done: *this is my baby*, you're thinking. My child is my life, my pride and joy; I live or die by his success.

Can you imagine the pressure your child has when they know what you think of yourself as a parent, a person, when your identified self-esteem is completely dependent on their grades, their graduation, their happiness, their feelings, their choices, their results, their life decisions, their standing on the athletic team. Some of you may know this feeling first-hand from your own parents.

It makes *me* want to rebel just thinking about it.

Lucky for you, I say to the teens (always in front of the parents), your parents may never get that they are already fabulous just as they are, despite their outcomes and life results. They may not have gone through the self-individuation process with their own parents. They may not, to this day, allow themselves to say no, speak their truth, or even know what they want for their own lives. So all that said, the best gift you can give yourself is to ignore what your parents are emphatically attached to and check within to see if this decision, whatever it is, is in your will, your highest good, your conscious self-reliance, your free choice.

Or are you shooting yourself in the foot by actually being controlled through your own chosen defiance?

Let's circle back to the idea of "no attachments." I know this concept is a tough one, so bear with me for a bit more explanation. I'm not saying that you'll never have battles with your child. You will, wherever you are attached to a particular issue. Your attachment to the issue is precisely what is likely to raise the level of defiance in your child!

So what are your attachment points? Make a list of the things that you are attached to, your non-negotiables. Hopefully, it will be a short list, because these are the battles you will most likely find yourself fighting. For the rest, for anything that's not on your short list, these are where, with compassion and understanding, you'll allow your child to explore his choices and desires, her wishes and wants.

And this will be a good thing, because the more your child exercises her voice, the better she will be at using it authentically and in her own best interest. From the child's perspective, the more I own my choices, the more accountability, ownership, and commitment I will have to my decisions. If I believe I can do it and you, the parent, don't, then I will get to prove to you that it *is* possible, even if I die trying. Hopefully, your child will be defiant about proving they can make straight A's even if you say it might be unreasonable to put that much pressure on yourself. This is your conscious free choice, not my life and my hard work.

For more information to help you handle your attachments to your child's decisions, see the *10 Keys to Compassion* section later in this book, or refer to the website. The next section will help you better understand your attachments and how to let go of that which is no longer serving you. As you understand your Inner Family, you will have the keys to unlock your irrational determination and personal defiance.

What is the Inner Family?

The Inner Family™ members represent the emotional developmental aspects of *you*. Many, if not all, of the "stories" we hold about our life have been created by the younger parts of ourselves. By understanding these young parts and by meeting their needs internally, those stories will no longer negatively impact or sabotage your life and the life you want to create.

2. Your Inner Family

Learning to understand and embrace each of these aspects of your own emotional development will allow you to compassionately fall in love with all of YOU!

Your Inner Family can be thought of as the emotional foundation of your Authentic Self. It can be the emotional foundation for everything that happens in your daily life. It is the core from which your desire to move forward from the space of wholeness, balance, and harmony can spring forth.

Self-recognition, self-awareness, healing, and growth all evolve from the development of your Inner Family.

Many of you are aware of the Inner Child work that has been popular over the past years. Some of you may have taken courses or weekend workshops to heal the wounded inner child. Most of these courses have focused on finding your little 2- or 3-year-old self, with all your emotional hurt feelings and learning to love and take care of your little, vulnerable inner child self.

Here, we will expand upon the Inner Child concept to include the Inner 7 Year Old and the Inner Teen. The addition of these increasingly older selves allows us to encompass not only the vulnerable and formative years of development, but also all of the spiritual, moral, mental, physical, sexual, and self-expressive aspects of development. Each of the increasingly older selves brings competing desires, as well as specific gifts, that when acknowledged and appreciated, allow us to express ourselves fully and authentically. We need this spectrum of voices from our Inner Family to guide us to our full potential.

The FUN journey we will be sharing together is not about whether you were loved or developed properly emotionally as a child. Instead, your Inner Family represents a series of emotional growth stages we *all* experienced and *continue to experience* during our lifetimes.

As you begin to recognize the difference between your Inner 3 Year Old, your Inner 7 Year Old and your Inner Teen, he or she will give voice to all the emotions, beliefs, and stories you are experiencing and/or have held on to throughout your life.

Characteristics of the Inner Family

The Inner 3 Year Old

The little scared, emotional, impulsive, expressive, vulnerable, raw child within us is our Inner 3 Year Old. This part of us is creative, energetic, and has a zest for life. Our Inner 3 Year Old dreams big, desires, wishes, has fantasies, and is joyful.

A wounded Inner 3 Year Old, who is often hidden, protected, and taken care of by our 7 year old, can be sad, mad, upset, internally focused, sees oneself as a victim, is needy, dependent, irresponsible, needs much attention, is consumed by the drama—totally into it, self-doubting, feeling deficient, has fears, all of them magnified and intense. I call this "having really big mixed feelings."

The Inner 3 Year Old has a close connection to your inner wise self. Many of us have learned or been told that it is not safe to feel, not safe to express, not safe even to know this vulnerable, raw part of ourselves. Sometimes it is hard to find, see, or feel the Inner 3 Year Old, because he or she is protected so well by our Inner 7 Year Old.

The Inner 7 Year Old

The Inner 7 Year Old is the moralist, parent-like, superhero, do-gooder, critic, know-it-all, hard worker, and the people-pleaser. This "feels really grown up" child can be externally focused, over-responsible, needing success, quite defensive, and very much a perfectionist. He or she is always right, as well as judgmental. The Inner 7 Year Old parades around just like an adult. I call this child the parentified adult. You may recognize this state in your own (external!) child, whenever he takes your inventory, tells you what to do, what to think, and tries to tell you how you should live or be as a parent.

Your Inner 7 Year Old is the one trying to get everything done, and as the rule-maker and rule-follower, works hard to keep everyone safe from risk and from playing too large.

My theory is that the vast majority of the time, 90 percent of the adult population lives and works as the structured, organized, rule-following, workaholic, perfectionist, overwhelmed, stressed-out Inner 7 Year Old.

Some percentage of these hardworking Inner 7 Year Olds are really emotional Inner 3 Year Olds pretending to be an all-grown-up Inner 7 Year Olds. You can spot an Inner 3 Year Old by the emotional outrage and exaggerated defensiveness. Look really hard to find the scared, vulnerable, hurt, sad little Inner 3 Year Old hiding behind the emotional tirade. You might even feel like you are being attacked by a self-righteous, entitled Teenager.

The Inner Teenager

The Inner Teen is the rule-breaker, the risk-taker, the exhibitionist who has the "teenager" attitude, is an idealist and a pessimist at the same time, and makes absolutely no logical or rational sense.

He or she judges self harshly while aspiring to be the superstar, football hero, and runway model. The Inner Teenager can't stand the mirror of anything off within himself that he sees in others. Inner Teens have a self-conscious body image, and/or an over-inflated body image, are irresponsible, yet expect to have it all given on a silver spoon. They have intense peer needs, yet desire freedom from all responsibility, are passionate, sexual, live for full self-expression, crave independence without cost or accountability. They blame others and have no respect for society's moral codes.

Recognize anyone??

Just as our Inner 7 Year Old protects our Inner 3 Year Old self, the Inner Teenager protects us from our perfectionist, workaholic Inner-7-Year-Old self. The Teenager is trying to protect our souls and trying to protect our life's purpose and passions.

Some percentages of Inner Teenagers are Inner 7 Year Olds pretending to be "cool teens." You can spot them by their moralistic, self-righteous indignation with a colorful, judgmental flair. Look hard at the happy-go-lucky attitude for the underlying worry and plan of attack for whatever may go wrong. You may see the worried, anxious Inner 7 Year Old that is working so hard to be seen dressed as, and acknowledged in, the "whatever, man" easy spirit of a teen.

How else can your Inner 7 Year Old come out? At the expense of being seen as a sexist, I've observed trends that happen in hundreds of couples. The woman has the responsibility of holding it together for the children, the family, and now most have their own jobs, as well. Many men are seen by disgruntled women as the fun dad, the irresponsible partner, the one that gets away with murder while the wife is "supposed" to hold everything together at home.

Even if their husbands are helpful with the children, women feel that ultimately the problems with the child are their problems to fix and make everything right, or they have failed as a mom, wife, and person. Men have the pressure of feeling they are really "the responsible breadwinner"—even if the wife brings in half the family income. If there are financial problems or if the spouse is unhappy with the children, most men feel it is ultimately their job to fix it and make everything right or they have failed as a husband, dad and person.

What's happening in this scenario is that the woman is acting the part of the Inner 7 Year Old, while the men act the part of the Inner Teen. What most women don't usually get is that the men are really being driven by their own, critical Inner 7 Year Olds, trying desperately to please their wives. When they can't win, they give up (just like your actual child does), and then the men play the acting-out Inner Teen role full tilt.

The Divine Wise Adult Self

The Divine Wise Self can be found by imagining your ideal, perfect parent, or future self. This is your truest self, the part of you that is intuitive, loving, positive, all-knowing, spirit-driven. This self is unconditionally accepting of all, accepting of what is in any given moment, relaxed, and peaceful, knowing everything is always Perfect and Divine. This self gets the big picture. It is a visionary, present in the moment, generous with love, gratitude, and meeting all internal needs abundantly, independently free, mature, selfless, self-loving, teachable, and open to learning. This self shares, owns and cleans up one's own stuff without competition and has undying faith and knowing it is all P & D: Perfect and Divine.

You may be asking yourself: *WHO? I don't have one of these in me.*

I challenge you to look and listen. You may first have to act as if you do, trust and know that you have an intuitive inner knowing that can help you manage this Inner Family cast of characters. It is through the 10 Key Process that you will meet and get to know your own inner family developmental states.

So now we've met the Inner 3 Year Old, the Inner 7 Year Old, the Inner Teen, and the Divine Wise Self.

What the heck do we do with them?

Once your Divine Wise Self has met the needs of the cast of characters, then the cast of characters is in alignment with the divine wise self, and that's when you'll find it easy and effortless to create, grow, and live your best life. This is when you can ask yourself the question, "How good can I stand it?"

Making Peace with your Inner Teen

At the heart of the journey, you are trying to protect the Inner 3 Year Old, your feelings and your passions. When you can get to the heart of your soul and make your little vulnerable Inner 3 Year Old feel safe, then your Inner 7 Year Old will feel like they have done their job protecting your Inner 3 Year Old and can then chill out, feeling accomplished. When your Inner 7 Year Old stops being so critical and judgmental, then your Inner Teenager will feel able to fully and passionately express itself.

One way to visualize this process is to imagine your healthy, loving, passionate Inner Teenager coming between your scared Inner 3 Year Old and your overly critical, overworked Inner 7 Year Old. Let the older sister or brother become your Inner Hero, your Inner Protector.

You're probably asking yourself right now "why are we worrying about *my* inner teen—it's my external real-to-life child that's making me crazy."

Here's the answer: when I make peace with my Inner Teen, I loooove yours. When I can't stand my Inner Teen, I also can't stand the reflection of mine in you.

As an experiment, give yourself permission to have a meltdown, to have a full range of the so-called negative emotions: rage, anger, upset, depression, sadness, greed, and give yourself permission to see what's perfect and real and authentic about all these feelings. If you do that, you'll also see how much fun it can be, and you'll begin to see that you *want* your children to play full-out as well. Then you get that they are awakening to their full life expression—and will not be doomed to a lifetime of workaholism or exhausted, resigned discontent.

So how do you make peace with your own Inner Teen?

It is essential to create peace between the Inner 7 Year Old and the Inner Teen. The Inner Teen is trying to keep us safe from our relentless, hard-working Inner 7 Year Old, and the Inner 7 Year Old cannot stand the Teenager, who keeps hijacking us and trying to sabotage us from achieving our ideal outcomes and life dreams.

A couple of examples:

- When your Inner 7 Year Old creates a diet plan to lose 15 pounds in a week and your Inner Teen sabotages it by seducing you to eat the entire chocolate cake...

The Inner 7 Year Old says:	The Inner Teen says:
I hate that I went off my diet again!	Screw society's perfect body image, I'll eat what I want, whenever I want it!

- Your Inner Teen wants to buy those sexy shoes you've been dying to get for months and your 7 year old has planned a 5-year budget to the penny, so your Inner Teen hijacks the credit card and goes on a shopping spree...

The Inner 7 Year Old says:	The Inner Teen says:
I can't stand that I can't live within my budgeted means.	There's more where that came from. The more I spend, the more money I'll make! Let's shop till we drop!

- Your Inner 7 Year Old has you working 14-hour days for ten days straight, and your Inner Teen hijacks you over lunch by getting you drunk, taking you to the beach for the rest of the day, and you end up losing your job...

The Inner 7 Year Old says:	The Inner Teen says:
I hate that I'm not doing it right...again.	Dude! I hated that job anyway. Let's par-tay!

The Inner 3 Year Old has other ways of acting out. You might find yourself hiding under the covers, crying, turning into a ball of mush. You might experience yourself in a fitful temper-tantrum rage with someone you don't even know, on the road or over the phone. This would be your Inner 3 Year Old hijacking your body and taking you out of the game altogether.

You can see how the exaggerated actions of the Inner 3 Year Old, the Inner 7 Year Old, and the Inner teen can present challenges for you! The good news is that your loving Adult Self can help mediate any one of these situations.

All children, the Inner 3 Year Old, the Inner 7 Year Old, and the Inner Teenager, need to be told by the loving Adult Self that they are not bad and not wrong, *no matter what*. At this point, your Inner 7 Year Old might be saying *well, that's just not right—there is no such thing as not being wrong, no matter what. The world could go crazy if we lived by that rule*!

Think of it this way: what if there was no way to screw up your life? What if there was no way to lose? What if there were no wrong answers? What if there was absolutely no way to fail?

These are beliefs you can choose to adopt. These are beliefs you can choose to accept.

And if you do, then I ask: how good can you stand it?

If you choose not to believe in failure, all your inner children will be doing exactly what they are developmentally meant to do. They will act out to awaken us to our unfulfilled emotional needs. If we work to fulfill those unmet needs, we will experience our full range of emotions and be afforded authentic self-expression.

When we fall in love with what is in any given moment, we create the opening for peace between the Inner 7 Year Old and the Inner Teenager. When this happens, the Inner Teen can fully and passionately express himself, the Inner 7 Year Old will chill out, feeling acknowledged and accomplished, and then the Inner 3 Year Old will feel safe enough to be vulnerable, raw, and totally authentic.

As you learn to recognize and listen to each of these emotional stepping stones that are represented by the members of your Inner Family, each part will feel heard and understood and safe. You will begin to feel unconditional love, compassion, and acceptance for all parts of yourself.

Once all parts of you are living in peace and harmony, you feel safe enough to take risks. You feel safe enough to begin living true to your authentic self. The result is that achieving your full potential becomes natural, effortless, and inevitable.

One of the goals of defining and sharing your story with yourself and others is to come to a sense of wholeness, that sense of completeness you have always desired. You are lovable, and everything in your life is and has been Perfect and Divine, no matter what life deals you.

So you may be thinking, I'm a survivor of incest, or my father died when I was five years old, my child was stillborn, etc. I'm not saying that your life is Perfect and Divine as a fact—I'm saying your life is Perfect and Divine *out of choice*. What has happened has happened. Life experiences have unfolded the way they have unfolded. Now the question is: what are you going to choose to do with that life experience? What are you going to choose to make it mean?

There is a famous motivational speaker, Toney Lineberry, who broke his neck, leaving left him permanently paralyzed from the chest down. He talks about this experience, which happened when he was 18, as one of the best gifts of his entire life. John Walsh, a parent many of us remember, had a child who was stolen and chose to transform the laws, and subsequently, the world. Many survivors of incest have chosen to take their experiences as opportunities to grow, share, and make a difference in the world.

I've asked hundreds of people to tell me the worst experience of their life. I then ask them who they are today because of that experience. What did they learn, what have they mastered, what are the golden nuggets—and the gifts and life lessons they describe are innumerable. It is a choice, not the truth.

What do you do with the rest of your life, given the experiences you have had? What if you choose to believe you were ruined, your life was a mistake, you are a mistake, you are a victim, and your life is one big failure...what happens next?

Or, what if you choose to believe your life is Perfect and Divine...*then what would you do next*?

One disclaimer here: don't go to Perfect and Divine until you are completely ready to experience bliss. Don't try this concept out until you are sick and tired of being sick and tired of being sick and tired. Until you are ready, play full-out where you are and love yourself up with all your big feelings, your fears, and thoughts of victimization. I'm not being sarcastic: I really invite you to turn up the victim full-blast, guilt and shame free. I choose to believe there is no way to do this wrong, not even staying in a space of total misery until you are ready to have it all. I fully admit there are times it is fun to roll around in this space just because I can, and also because I know I can leave it when I'm ready.

Identifying Your Inner Family Members

To help you become acquainted with your Inner Family, find pictures of yourself when you were about 3 years old, 7 years old, and as a teenager. Refresh your memory of who you were at these ages. Many times, just by looking into your own eyes as a child, you can tap into those long-lost feelings and emotions.

Also, find a picture of yourself as your Divine Wise Adult Self. This can be an actual photograph of yourself or a picture you might find in a book or magazine that exemplifies your vision of a Divine Wise Adult being your ideal, loving self.

It can be helpful, and is also fun, to give names to your different emotional ages. I have given my Inner Family the follow names: Little B (age 3), Super B (age 7), Bubblin' B (teen), and Dr. B (Divine Wise Woman). Again, having a picture in front of you may be helpful when choosing a name that fits.

Most of all...have FUN! There is no way to do this right, there is no way to do this wrong, and absolutely *no way* to screw this up.

Needs			
Inner 3 Year Old	**Inner 7 Year Old**	**Inner Teenager**	**Divine Wise Adult**
To be loved and hugged	To be safe, secure	To be seen and adored	No needs
To feel any and all feelings	Be accomplished	Speak the truth	Has everything internally given
Not to be fixed or corrected, just held	Structure	You can't screw this up	Sourced by all
Needs attention	Organization	To be messy	To live your blueprint
To be safe, protected, secure	Clarity	Full self-expression	Experience life
Positive reinforcement	Focus	Free to be me	
Calm, Comfort	It is all taken care of	Need to have fun	
To be cared for	There is an adult present	Guilt-free play	
Wise Woman/Wise Man Guidance	Someone is taking care of everything	Want to let go of control	
Reassurance	They can go play, everyone is okay	Live in the unknown	
To know that nobody gets to be bad	"No one gets to be wrong"	"There's no way to screw this up"	

Characteristics			
Inner 3 Year Old	**Inner 7 Year Old**	**Inner Teenager**	**Divine Wise Adult**
Emotional, Young Feelings, Raw Feelings	Mental, Critical Thinking	Physical, passionate	Spiritual part of self
Has closest connection to Spiritual Body	Has closest connection to Mind Body	Has closest connection to Physical Body	Is Pure Spirit, Pure Love
Dependent, needy, wants everyone to do it for them	Counter-dependent; Not willing to accept help	Inter-dependent/ Independent; Free spirit	Total Acceptance of all developmental ages
Very vulnerable	Self-righteous; Know-it-all to cover insecurities	Cool & collected mixed with passion & rage	Absolute inner and all-knowingness
Magical thinking, dreamer, optimist	Intelligent, Meticulous, Pessimist	Idealist, Brilliant, Innovative, Outspoken	Realist, Mediator, Your Highest God Self
Lovable, Craves attention, Affectionate, Snuggly	Conditional love, Guarded, Defensive	Expressive, Passionate, Craves approval	Unconditional love; Fully able to receive and give
Blind trust, Undiscerning, Indiscriminate, Naïve	Distrusts, Skeptical, Hyper-vigilant	Questions authority, Self-doubting, Lacking confidence	Trust in Self, Others, ALL
Unruly, Out-of-control, Irrational, Unaware	Follows the rules, Sets goals, Rational, Compliant	Breaks the rules, Defiant, Rebellious, Risk-takers	Creates rules that serve the highest good in order to win
Unintentionally messy, Disorganized	Perfectionist, Meticulous, Organized	Intentionally Messy, Irresponsible, Wild	Knows everything is Perfect & Divine as is

Characteristics			
Inner 3 Year Old	**Inner 7 Year Old**	**Inner Teenager**	**Divine Wise Adult**
Immature emotional full-out expression, Excitable	Stunted emotional expression	Irrational, Medicated emotional expression	Can hold all emotional expressions of all ages
Curious, Spontaneous, Funny, Playful, Creative	Judging, Critic, Controlling, Competitive	Saboteur, Addict, Brazen, Fearless	Source and guided by the universe/God
Center of attention, Self-centered	Superhero, Wants to save the world, Protective	Superstar, Sexual, Social, Lazy, Adventurous	Ideal parent of Inner Family

Motivations			
Inner 3 Year Old	Inner 7 Year Old	Inner Teenager	Divine Wise Adult
Praise, Love, Attention	Acknowledgement	Being seen and adored	Experiences of Inner Family members
Creative projects	Independent projects	Team projects	Unconditional love for Inner Family members
Movement, Dance	Feeling useful	Challenges	Gives selflessly to Inner Family members
Music, Singing	Accomplishments, Completion	Being part of decision-making	Wisdom of other Wise Selves
New experiences	Knowing how to win	Choices, options on how to win/play/be involved	Gaining greater self-awareness
Affection, Cuddling	Negative avoidance (fear, pain, punishment)	Peers	Full self-expression of Divine Self

Triggers			
Inner 3 Year Old	**Inner 7 Year Old**	**Inner Teenager**	**Divine Wise Adult**
Being alone, Being ignored	Irresponsible teen behavior	Know-it-all 7-year-old	Nothing and no one
Critical 7-year-old	Irrational 3-year-old behavior	Embarrassing, emotional, 3-year-old	If triggered, it is a young part of you
High-risk teen	Disorganization	Not getting to live his dreams	Is akin to saying 'What would trigger God?'
Fighting	Confusion	Feeling forced to play small	
Not feeling safe and cared-for	Not-knowing	Boredom, lack of stimulation	
Loud noises	Not feeling purposeful	Feeling left out by peers	
Confusion	Not being able to win	Not being in the club	
Basic needs not being met (sleep, food, shelter)	Not feeling accomplished	Being told what and when to do anything	
Being made bad-and-wrong	Chaos, Lack of order	When told they are wrong or bad	

Connect with Your Inner Family

Your Inner Family™ is an important part of building and understanding how you work. Your Inner Family is your core foundation. These inner players are the powerful creators of what you desire, how you are being, and how you react to life and others. The more intimate you become with your Inner Family and the better you know how to meet the emotional needs of each age, the more emotionally balanced you will become. This will create more harmony in your life, allowing you access to more of your authentic personal power, unconditional self-acceptance, and inner joy.

> **Helpful Hint...**
> Use a different writing instrument to represent the voice of each member of your Inner Family. You might use a crayon for your 3 yr old and a calligraphy pen for your Wise Self.

Now, let's take a look at what each member of your Inner Family needs most right now. Let's also look each member's concept of an "ideal" family.

Take a moment and allow yourself to connect with each member of your Inner Family. Listen carefully as you ask each member the following questions. Write down whatever answer you receive, without changing the wording. There is no right or wrong answer. Allow yourself to accept whatever arises without judgment.

See below for one possible example. Trust yourself...when you ask these questions, you will hear an answer. Trust that what you hear is perfect and divine *for you*. Remember there is NO WAY to do this wrong! Have fun with this process and let yourself play with possible answers.

1. What do you think you need most for each member of Your Inner Family?

3 year old

_____

_____

_____

_____

7 year old

_____

_____

_____

_____

Teen

_____

_____

_____

_____

Wise Self

_____

_____

_____

_____

2. Describe the "Ideal" family for each member of Your Inner Family.

   3 year old

   _____

   _____

   _____

   _____

   7 year old

   _____

   _____

   _____

   _____

   Teen

   _____

   _____

   _____

   _____

   Wise Self

   _____

   _____

   _____

   _____

3. Describe the "Ideal" child for each member of Your Inner Family.

   3 year old

   _____

   _____

   _____

   _____

   7 year old

   _____

   _____

   _____

   _____

   Teen

   _____

   _____

   _____

   _____

   Wise Self

   _____

   _____

   _____

   _____

4. Describe the "Ideal" parent for each member of Your Inner Family.

3 year old

_____

_____

_____

_____

7 year old

_____

_____

_____

_____

Teen

_____

_____

_____

_____

Wise Self

_____

_____

_____

_____

If you're finding this exercise daunting, an example is available at the back of the book.

Meet Your Inner Family

How do you identify the parts of your Inner Family in yourself? Let me give you some examples.

Inner 3 Year Old

I was sitting in Starbucks, talking with a friend, and a little girl with those roller-skate sneakers went right by me and blooped me in the side. She just nailed me, and I screamed and said, "Whoa!" The child just kept on walking, so I said, "Hey! What are you doing?" and the child didn't even turn around. Her mother and her friend walked right by and missed the entire interaction, but all of it made me laugh and smile while I loved up my Inner 3 Year Old spirit.

That's the Inner 3 Year Old free spirit:
fun-loving, full of self-expression, impulsive
can have a total temper tantrum and
then come right back out of it in two seconds flat.

Inner 7 Year Old

I think of the Inner 7 Year Old as an alter-ego of us that was developed to protect the vulnerable, inner child. So the Inner 7 Year Old is like a parentified, petrified, miniature, pretending-to-be adult, and this alter-ego is in every single one of us. You can find an Inner 7 Year Old in a know-it-all two-year-old. You can find it in a pressured, perfectionist teenager, and if you look really hard, you might find the Inner 7 Year Old in your controlling, manipulative, nagging spouse...and if you're willing to be authentic, vulnerable, you just might find it in your hard-working, super-duper hero, trying-to-get-it-right self.

> *The Inner 7 Year Old is the perfectionist, the workaholic, the moralist, the I-got-to-do-it-right-or-I'm-going-to-die, and no matter what, that little know-it-all will always be with you.*

Inner Teenager

The Inner Teenager is the part of you that is passionate, your voice that is connected to your passionate spirit and your life's purpose. The inner teenager is like your soul. This is the part of you that gives you permission to speak the truth, and will tell you flat-out anything you want to say, like *you're ugly and you dress funny.* Your inner teen speaks your authentic, politically incorrect truth, and is the one who says, "You know, I wouldn't do that if I were you," or "That makes you look fat," when no one asked for your opinion, much less gave you permission to take someone's personal inventory.

Your Inner Teen is the one that sits on the couch eating bon-bons, even though you're on a strict diet. Your Inner Teen takes you shopping and buys you shoes you're never going to wear, even though you can't afford them—just because you deserve it for all those hours and hours you were overworked and underappreciated.

The seven-year-olds may think they're doing the right thing, but they don't have the vision. They don't have the big picture. The seven-year-olds want to drive, but they can't see over the steering wheel and out the proverbial windshield.

> *Your Inner Teen is your truth-teller,*
> *can believe in and create anything.*
> *Your Inner Teen is the one who has the*
> *vision for your future, your idealistic vision and*
> *life's purpose.*

Divine Wise Adult

Now, if some of you are saying, "Oh my gosh, I don't want to let my life be run by a three- or seven-year-old, or worse, a teen!," lucky for you, there's another option. I call this person the Divine Wise Self, and this is like the parent, the inner parent, the ideal self that you can actually tap into. The Divine Wise Self becomes the parent of these three characters, so that all three get their voice. The Inner 3 Year Old gets to feel safe, the Inner 7 Year Old gets to feel successful, and the Inner Teen gets to feel seen and known and free to present himself the way he wants to.

> *The Divine Wise Adult is your greatest friend,*
> *your mentor, leader, cheerleader, Inner Family*
> *facilitator and collaborator,*
> *This part is all-knowing for what is best for YOU,*
> *all loving all forgiving,*
> *and believing in you no matter what.*
> *You will always be loved, seen, and held*
> *with Divine, loving hands: YOURS.*

How Does Each Member of the Inner Family Relate to Teenology?

When I talk about teen energy and Teenology, I'm talking about the teen in all of us. So it's worth taking a minute to understand what defiance—teen or otherwise—provides for us.

Defiance is a process of finding one's voice. If you have been run by and living through your compliant, do-gooder, Inner 7 Year Old, the only way to find your truth is to give yourself permission to question the status quo, question authority, question "the way we've always done it," question facts you've known forever, question what society, and particularly, your parents, believe to be "right" for your life.

It is through giving yourself permission to question what is, being willing to play with being "wrong," and surrendering to the possibility that there may be other possibilities, that you find your own, authentic voice. If you are not able or willing to go here, you are most likely stuck developmentally in the quagmire of perfectionism, secure in the one "right" way for everyone. If you are not willing to sit, even temporarily, in the unknown, or entertain the possibility that you don't have all the answers, how will you begin to grow, learn, or develop into new possibilities?

So, if a parent acts like a little know-it-all seven-year-old (and most of us usually do!), she will trigger everyone around them to be a defiant Inner Teen.

If I tell you: "Do your homework. Hand me your wallet. Make up your bed. Get off the phone. Brush your teeth," I'm also saying: *think the way I think because I said so, and I know more than you do and what's right for you and your life, and you are an idiot to not know to do these things for yourself. You can't think for yourself; I must remind you of everything to keep you safe because I'm all-knowing and you are an idiot.*

Does it make the hair on the back of your neck stand up? Imagine someone like your parent, your spouse, or your boss doing that to you (and most authoritarian bosses usually do!).

Even children acting from their own inner seven-year-olds can make their parents' inner teens become defiant!

Child (Inner 7 Year Old) says to Mom:	Mom's Inner Teen says back:
Mom, why are you wearing that?	Why? Are you my fashion expert now?

Husband (Inner 7 Year Old) says to Wife:	Wife's Inner Teen says back:
Did you really need to buy one more pair of shoes?	Yes! And now that you mentioned it, I'm going to go buy 10 more!!

Wife (Inner 7 Year Old) says to Husband:	Husband's Inner Teen says back:
You said you'd do the dishes...are you just going to sit there on the couch?	Yes, as a matter of fact, I am. In fact, I'm not even going to respond to you at all. "Oh. Are you talking to me?"

Can you see how the Inner Teen shows up in the adult, shows up in the seven-year-old, shows up in the teens, the twenties, and so on?

If you are not aware of when you move in and out of these states—when you are in a three-year-old puddle of mush, when you're in a know-it-all-seven-year-old state, when you are in a rebellious, defiant because-I-said-so-and-I'm-the-center-of-the-universe teenage state—you can hurt feelings or quickly turn a bad situation worse. It might be easier to start looking for these states in others first.

When you are in your Divine Wise Self, you're actually noticing that it's okay to feel what you feel, it is okay for you to have needs, and you're okay with others' needs, and not necessarily your responsibility to meet those needs. Your Divine Wise Self trusts your children to have their own inner voices, trusts your spouse to have his own inner voice, and best of all, is learning to trust your own inner voice.

It's when we start second-guessing, challenging, defying our relationships, including our relationship with ourselves, that we act contrary to our own best interests and shoot ourselves in the foot.

All right, you may be thinking this is all well-and-good...but when it comes down to it and my child doesn't pick up her laundry off the floor and dad doesn't get up and help with the dishes, then who does it?

You're right...Mom, usually. Mom is the glue that holds the family together in many cases, makes it work...traditional and stereotypical, I'm sure, and I hear about it and I see it in action every day.

So turn that around and you can see that of all the people in the house, the mom, potentially, is the one for whom most of her needs are going un-met.

If you're a mom nodding her head, how's that working for you? Are you tired of being the super-duper perfect do-gooder 7 Year Old? Are you ready to let someone else get some of the credit and fun of being the superstar?

We've all heard the expression, "If you always do what you've always done, you will always get what you've always gotten." In other words, if you keep doing the same thing but you expect a different outcome, that is the definition of insanity.

If I gave you a hundred dollars every single day, would you take it and spend it? Why not? Is it my responsibility for giving you the money and expecting something different, or should you, in your infinite wisdom, say, "Oh no, don't give me that $100 to spend on anything I want with absolutely no consequences and knowing there will be an endless supply and another $100 tomorrow"?

Who is the one who keeps doing all the work? Who is the one who keeps reinforcing the less-than-desirable behavior? Are you willing and ready to take ownership for what you have created and positively reinforced? Remember, no one gets to be wrong, not even you, or me for making you feel bad-and-wrong. It is through this playful possibility that you could actually take your life back.

If so, you have the ability to transform your situation. If you are waiting for everyone else to awaken and say stop taking care of me, stop giving me $100, stop giving and giving and giving, you will be sadly disappointed.

That does not mean you need to stop having the need or the desire that everyone will conform to your wishes. It just means that if you expect it to be done when, where, and how you need it to be completed for your immediate happiness, you may live a very miserable, frustrated life.

Expectations vs. Reality

What do you expect of others?

The more aligned your Expectations become with the Reality of what is, the less stress you will experience. The difference between your expectations and your perception of reality is equal to the amount of stress you will feel in your life. If you have HUGE expectations versus your perception of reality, you will experience a HUGE amount of stress in your life. There are two ways to reduce this kind of stress:

- improve the reality of what is—my guess is that you have already attempted to do all you could possibly do on this front.

- lower or change your expectations—accept what is currently happening as Perfect & Divine.

In what ways can you make smaller steps to achieve your expectations? What can you control? Is it easier to control others or to control yourself? How's it been working for you so far?

What are ways you can give yourself what you need? You can attempt to internally and externally give yourself all of what you want and need. You can attempt to ask for what you want, knowing there will be times it is perfect for someone to meet your needs because it happens to be their truth, as well. It will also be perfect at times for someone to stand in their power and allow you to master the experience of accepting their no, or stretching and learning how to do "it" for yourself, or giving another person a chance to meet that need and be the superhero this time.

There's also another alternative, one I think of as a lost art: visualization. You can give yourself the edification, the visualization, of the fulfilling experience you desire. That visualization can help you meet your inner need.

And what I have found is that as I give the love, compassion, and acceptance, as I meet the inner need, it manifests externally in my outer world almost by MAGIC!

Why not try this: for one day, ask for what you want, knowing the other person always has the right to say NO. Let's walk through the possible outcomes to your request.

If the other person feels your request is a demand, you will most likely receive a defiant response. For example, someone may say, "Sure, I'll do that," (maybe even having totally pure intentions from their 7-year-old self) and then lo-and-behold they forgot, overslept, had something come up, maybe even woke up with a stomachache—no doubt you have heard these excuses.

If the other person says no, then what? If your happiness is dependent on controlling another person, again you quite possibly will live a very unhappy life. I taught listening, assertion, problem solving, decision making, managing conflict for corporations for years. I have found that even with the greatest of skill, the most respectful request, and the honorable intention of a win-win solution—sometimes people refuse to do what you want, even if it is for their own good!

So if we can't ultimately control others, how do we create bliss, and live into happiness in all this gray?

Where Do You Put Your Focus?

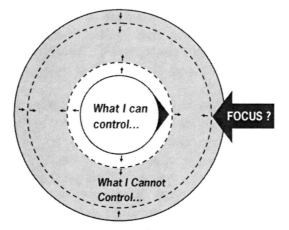

If you focus on the outside circle, what you cannot control, the inside circle gets smaller and smaller and you feel more out of control.

What do you have absolutely no control over? Others, weather, corporate management, spouses, customers, children, dogs, society, politics, etc.

If you focus on the inside of the circle—what you can control—YOU—the smaller circle gets larger and larger, impacting the outside circle and making you feel more and more in control of your world. It is actually through focusing on YOU and what you can control that you have more impact in what you have no control over.

What do you have control over? Your thoughts, your reactions, your behavior, your feelings, etc. Basically, only YOU! Where do you choose to put your focus?

Parent and Make Peace with YOUR Inner Teen

This is actually easier than you can possibly imagine. It is so simple and so easy, yet the only way you will be able to do this is to be willing to be totally wrong about everything that you've learned from your entire life.

It is absolutely possible, it's absolutely simple, but you have to be *willing to be wrong*. And I know this idea can be difficult to parse. For some of you, I might as well have said, "You only need to cut off your right arm."

If you're the kind of person who has a story from your seven-year-old self that your spouse doesn't pick up after himself, he leaves the toilet seat up, he can't figure out how to get the dishes from the sink to the dishwasher.... even if and especially if you have years and years of evidence gathered...

Or if you have a story that your youngest child is a lazy, no-good son-of-a-gun...even if and especially if you have proof...

Or your daughter is a smarty-pants with an attitude, and is here to make your life a living hell...even if and especially if you have a video, and *your* mother asks you why you let her get away with that...

Or that your boss is out to ruin you and take you to the bottom of the pit...even if and especially if you could ask a hundred people and they would all take your side and totally agree with you...

Then you get to be right.

Being right just may be the most deadly, addictive, powerful drug on the market. Being right is comforting. Being right gives us the illusion of and sense of safety. Being right gives us the ability not to take responsibility for our lives, our experiences, our creations, our results and impacts. Being right gives us someone else to blame for anything and everything that is not working in our lives.

If you get to be right, you will lead those people, like your son, daughter, spouse, and boss described above, exactly and perfectly into the horrific story in your head.

But let's look at the downside of being right all the time.

If your husband jumps every time you say "how high," there will be no passion and you will feel you are married to a compliant, passionless three-year-old with no testicles.

If your son jumps every time you say "how high," he will learn how to comply with not only you, but the drug dealer and all his high school peers, the over-controlling girlfriend or wife, and the boss who will work your child to a pulp.

If your daughter does not learn how to say no, how to be someone other than a nice, compliant, respectful, good girl and jump when you say "how high," she will also learn to be nice to people who abuse her physical and emotional space.

I can't say yes to your request without an option to say NO. You can't trust my yes, and *I* can't trust my yes unless it is okay, a possibility, safe for me to even entertain a NO. Of course, we all have a right to say no. Of course, we all have the ability to say no. Of course, we all CAN say no. Or can we? Can you?

So here's the trick.

In order to parent these inner states, you have to have absolutely no demands, no desire, no need, and no expectations for any ONE specific person to be responsible to fill you up on the outside, right now, on your 3-year-old impulsive want-what-you-want timeframe. Instead, you create an inner and outer village of support. You become the teacher, the lover, the spouse, the partner, the healer, the leader—everything—for your own inner family.

What does the Inner 3 Year Old need?

See chart page 48.

What does the Inner 7 Year Old need?

See chart page 48.

What does the Inner Teen need?

See chart page 48.

Provide for Your Inner Family

Let's take a minute and do an exercise. You might want somebody else to read this to you.

Close your eyes. See your Inner 3 Year Old, your Inner 7 Year Old, and your Inner Teenager. Maybe you see them in a pool, swimming around, or you can see them sitting on the couch, lying in your bed. All that matters is that you can be at peace and let them show up.

A lot of times, if people have been battling, at war with their Inner Family, they will see their kids in separate corners with their arms folded. Sometimes they'll find their little Inner 3 Year Old in the tearful puddle, hiding under the bed or in the closet.

When you can see all three, you are in your Divine Wise Self. I call this going to the 30,000-foot view.

If you can only see the three-year-old, and you're disgusted by his vulnerability, you're probably seven. If you can only see the inner seven-year-old and you *hate* that know-it-all kid, you're probably the teenager.

If you can see the teenager, see the seven-year-old, and see the three-year–old, you might want to have the teenager go stand between the other two inner children. This way, your seven-year–old can't keep beating up your little three-year-old. Let your tough, teen voice stand between the two and be the protector of these two younger states.

Now imagine the Inner Wise Self talking to all three and asking the three-year-old, "What do you need to feel safe today?"

And then listen, no matter how crazy it might make you feel.

If your Inner 3 Year Old says: "I want to be in your arms," put her into your arms and fast-forward in time so she has the experience of being in your arms as long as she needs to be: days, weeks, months, decades, as long as she wants until she is ready to jump down. Give her more time than she could possibly want.

If they say they want ice cream, give them an entire buffet of all they can eat ice cream with chocolate sauce and everything that they ever want to fill up their little emotional tummies. Whatever your little three-year-old needs and wants—a princess outfit, a gun and holster, a curly slide, a swimming pool, whatever they want—give it to your little Inner 3 Year Old in vivid detail. Then go to your seven-year-old and ask what she needs to finally and ultimately feel successful.

What do they need? They may say: I need ribbons, I need awards, I need money, I need praise and accolades...whatever you're hearing they may need, give it to them! Put them up on stage, or put them up front of their peers in the 2nd grade class and tell them how wonderful they are. Have the whole class give them a standing ovation, a blue ribbon, and a certificate that tells them once and for all they are good enough, they are complete, they have caught the carrot, and are fully accomplished just as they are in this moment.

They are complete. They are fabulous exactly as they are. When that child feels filled up more than anything he could possibly want or need, then go to the teenager. Ask your teenager: "What is your heart's desire? What do you want to be known for? How do you want to be seen? What do you want to bring to the world?"

And *listen*. Because no matter what your teen asks for, it is within your power to provide that internal comfort.

Give them whatever they need to feel powerful and empowered and confident and inspired and *fabulous* about themselves. It is by fulfilling all these unmet emotional needs that you will be able to give the same thing to your real-life child in real-time. And, if you are filled up by meeting your own emotional needs, you will no longer need your child to grow up early, becoming your parentified adult, because you never had a divine, wise adult as your parent. As you meet your own inner emotional needs, you model for your child how to meet their own inner needs at an age-appropriate stage. The result? A win for everyone, because they will not need addictive behavior, peers, or your undivided attention to fulfill their every emotional need.

In conclusion, make a duplicate of your Divine Wise Self for each Inner Family Member, and allow your Divine Wise Self to give and give and give to each age and tell them you will all come together often to listen and understand what they need and have to say.

On a challenging note: now let me say something you've probably never thought before. All those negative experiences you've endured, the ones that caused you deep hurts and emotional bruises and scars? *Those "negative" experiences were a gift.*

Because you've lived through them, you are stronger, smarter, more resilient, more empathetic...the list goes on.

If I asked you if you would want to erase those so-called negative experiences from your existence, but you'd have to give up all those gifts you'd received as a result, what would you say?

So it is through this personal journey of fulfilling your young inner selves' emotional needs that you are then able to embrace new possibilities of life.

EMBRACING DEFIANCE

If you are afraid of love because you have been hurt, you keep yourself safe, withdrawn, and protected from new experiences. If you can't deal with failure and stories you have about how you blew it because you didn't go to college, married too early, had a child before you were ready, or a million other stories, then you keep yourself safe by avoiding: new career paths, publishing your songs, meeting the person of your dreams, writing your book, starting your new business, traveling the world—or whatever dream you are choosing to avoid.

And here is the big huge stick I use with parents. Brace yourself. If you are afraid of living, recording, writing, traveling, loving, then your child will most likely live into your same life story.

(That's how much they want to please you.)

The following example brings this home. When I was preparing to record my music CDs, an incredible musician and father of four helped me prepare for the recording studio. He was envious and blown away that I had written my music and planned to record in less than six months. I challenged him by saying that the question is not how could I do such a bodacious thing, but why hadn't he recorded yet, given your gifts, abilities, and the beautiful music he had written.

He said, "I have not perfected my music as of yet."

His youngest, incredibly gifted child of fourteen years came into the basement to play with us. I asked him what he planned to do with his musical abilities.

He said, "You know, I'm sure I'll be like my dad, playing and writing music in the garage."

The next child came in, and I asked the same thing. Again, same answer. I looked at the dad, and he said, "I get it, I get it."

Two weeks later, I heard the father was in the studio recording his music and guess who was there with him—all four children!!

The goal is to go through your entire life and say without a shadow of a doubt, *I have no regrets*!!

How do I Integrate my Inner Teen into My Life?

It is through asking, listening, and meeting the emotional needs of your young selves that your Inner Teen is even given permission to dream, visualize, and live you into your life's passions. If your Inner 3 Year Old does not feel safe in the world, then your Inner 7 Year Old will be very protective and defensive, keeping you very small and hiding out under the proverbial covers.

If your Inner 7 Year Old never feels like she can do enough, do it right, she can't win, or she's always failing, then she will play it small, stay in the stands, and never really play full-out. If you are willing to let your Inner Teen have a voice, say the unthinkable, if only in your private journal or to a safe friend, then you will become aware of your Inner Teen's passions, dreams, and ideal visions.

If you are willing to give yourself permission to fall on your face, tell yourself that there is no way to fail, then you will be able to have new life experiences, experience bliss beyond your wildest dreams, and propagate that forward by giving your real-life children the idea that anything is possible.

So the story goes, if you put a colony of fleas in a jar, they learn to jump just short of the lid. When you take the lid off the jar, nothing changes. They continue to jump just short of where the lid had been. If, by chance, one flea jumps beyond the former lid position, the rest of the fleas will immediately follow. As a parent, you have the ability to go beyond what your parents were ever able or willing to do, and as you do, your children will be right behind you.

Also—so the story goes—if a frog jumps into a pot of boiling water, he will immediately jump out as fast as he jumped in. However, if the frog is swimming around in a cold pot and the temperature is slowly raised, the frog will never jump out of the pot. Again, as the parent, you can make note of the comfort zone your parents, you, and your children have been living into. If you notice that your past stories, your generational patterns, are frying your happiness, then by all means, jump out of the boiling pot!

It will be your crazy, wild, irrational, high-risk Inner Teen that will be the first to notice, name, and have the audacious idea to jump out of the intergenerational pot that may have been cooking your family for decades.

3. The 10 Keys to Compassion

Wh at do you think of when you think of compassion?

Many people hold the belief that compassion is something you give to others. For example, you take care of your children first, sacrifice yourself for the sake of the whole, be nice to others at your own expense, put yourself last, service is selfless, if you don't have anything nice to say, don't say anything at all, keep your mouth shut, take only what you need to survive...how many of these thoughts bob around in your head throughout the day?

I am inviting you to consider the possibility of throwing all these beliefs out the window and open yourself to a new paradigm that may literally rock your world and turn you inside out and upside down.

The 10 Keys to Compassion is a template, tools, and concepts to help you fall madly in love with yourself, just as you are in this exact moment, to experience more joy than you ever thought possible, and to step you into your greatness, so that you can pass your gifts onto others and help others to achieve and find their gifts.

The 10 Keys to Compassion are tools to make sense of and understand pain, suffering, big feelings, and transform them into compassion, love, and playfulness.

The 10 Keys to Compassion are a step-by-step process that can be applied to every aspect of one's life: health, wealth, relationships, parenting, self-growth, and business.

Let me reiterate that the 10 Keys education, concepts, and support process allow you to make peace with your past hurt, pain, fears, and destructive patterns, so that your children don't have to relive your past. You get to create a new story for you and your children to live into, so that your life is filled with less stress, less drama, and more fun, compassion, love, and playfulness.

Compassion is the Key to Life

The compassion I'm referring to here is compassion for the self.

I like myself just fine, you say. But let's look deeper. Why is compassion for the self important?

A child is born needing love, care, and soothing at all hours of the day and night. Sometimes the parent is emotionally and physically depleted and has nothing to give to the child. It is in this moment, and moments like these, that the love, tolerance, patience, acceptance, and compassion you can give yourself are essential. If you have to give when you are depleted, you may blame the child for your own emptiness and exhaustion. The child then feels she is causing the depletion of her caregiver, and ultimately, because she needs anything at all from you, that there is something wrong with herself at the core of her being.

When you take care of yourself first, you no longer need your real-life child to be perfect, happy, together, make good grades, etc., for your sake and well being.

An example, I've asked hundreds of children if they would prefer their parent tell them yes to a request and become angry with the child, or to tell them no and allow the child to become angry and disappointed with the parent. One hundred percent of the time, the child says they would rather be the one angry. Parents tell me the same thing. They say it is so hard to say no, to disappoint their child, and deal with their wrath and the subsequent big feelings.

Someone has to have the tools to deal with the other person's *no*. One way the child learns is by modeling your response to his no and standing in your truth when you would prefer to say no. It is through your boundaries that your child learns new life lessons, like the life-skills to get a job because he wants to be able to buy what he wants when he wants it. With your no, your child gets to work for what he wants and earn it, instead of feeling guilty for taking you to the poorhouse and you losing your home, increasing your credit debt, or otherwise depleting you physically and financially.

An extreme example, to be sure, but what they tell you on the airplane is true: put your mask on first, then adjust your child's. Otherwise, your child will feel he is responsible for depleting you and he OWES you his life, which, of course, he can never catch up or repay.

If we expect our children to meet our high expectations and fix our disappointments, well, that's a lot of pressure on a child to take care of you and your emotional needs.

One of the biggest causes of pain is when we expect, wish, want everything to be different now than whatever is currently happening in our life. For example, we want a hundred grand in the bank and then we would be happy. Or we want to be 30 pounds lighter. Or we want our house to be remodeled, clean, organized, or we want our children to make a 4.0 GPA. Or we want our partner to do that thing we need done now because we have said something a hundred times and they never listen.

Or we need _____ (fill in the blank).

What would give you happiness, right now in this moment? What would give you a sense of calm, peace, joy, love, satisfaction with life as you know it?

The 10 Keys to Compassion program helps you to fall madly in love with who you are and where you are right now, at this perfect age and stage of your life. The program helps you see what is perfect about your reactions, your feelings, your current life stories and creations with no blame, no shame, and TONS of love and compassion. Protected by the armor that comes with love, you will be able to face your biggest challenges with strength, courage, and playfulness.

What Does a Life Look Like Without the 10 Keys?

Are you up for another example?

Let me tell you about my life without the 10 Keys. At age 29, I was up until 2 o'clock in the morning, putting together a presentation for my first $1,000 keynote gig (getting things together at the last minute was part of my family's intergenerational pattern), and I was hit head-on by a drunk driver. I went to the hospital, and all I could think about was: how do I get to my presentation the next morning? How am I going to live without that thousand dollars, and what am I going to do, because I had a two-week ski vacation scheduled for three days away. So as they took the heart-monitoring wires and plugs off me, I asked five specialists if I could still go skiing.

They all laughed at me.

I had over 50 stitches on my forehead and my lip, and my ankle was sprained and in a splint. I had bruises all over my body. They had to cut me out of my own truck just to get me to the hospital.

I looked at the doctors and said, "No, I'm serious. Can I go snow skiing in three days?"

I was in *scarcity*; I had in my mind, in my little, myopic world, that it was the last time I would get to go on a two-week snow ski vacation for the rest of my life, ever. Obviously, there was no Divine Wise Self in the building that day, no internal caregiver looking out for me. And by the way, I was on a plane three days later and even attempted to ski.

So that's one example of what happens when there's no Divine Wise Self on board and your inner children and inner teen are running your life.

Can you think of an example from your own life? What are your Inner Children and Inner Teen doing while you are not present to your Divine Wise Self?

What are the 10 Keys?

Compassion	How to bring peace and joy to yourself as a parent and as a person. Having compassion for yourself, where you are, in this moment.
Own Your Story	Informs how you behave, relate, and the results you will have in the world. Consciously creating the "stories" about your life, or the stories you want to live into, in your life.
Mirror, Mirror	How to create and own the Divine reflection of what you are certain you see in another. (This also includes the other person's intentions.) Awareness or possibility that everything you perceive is a reflection of self.
Playful-Messy	Messiness as your fun factor. If you are not making a mess, you are playing way too small. Willingness to play full-out and make a mess in order to have it all.
Affect	Feel Your Feelings (Feel it, or you will ACT IT OUT!) Fully express your feelings, so you don't unconsciously act them out.
Self-Care	Give to yourself from abundance or spread desperation and emptiness. Giving ourselves what we need to feel fulfilled inside and out.
Self-Trust	Listen to, integrate, and follow all your inner voices. Be your word. Rely on your own inner resources with confidence.

Internal/External Focus	Inspire Questions versus Unmet Demands. Manifest "Ideal" thoughts and beliefs, whatever is "Ideal" for you.
Organize Your Village	Build support for your Inner Teen that lasts a lifetime. Create support systems Internally and Externally.
kNOw Your Boundaries	Can I trust your Yes? Can you trust your No? Set clear and loving boundaries.

Working with the 10 Keys process takes a willingness to open your eyes...a willingness to reduce, or ideally, remove, your attachment to the idea of *should*. It takes an acceptance that you are where you are developmentally, and we move forward from here. If you make yourself bad-and-wrong for not knowing about any blind spots you might discover, or about where those blind spots are in you, then you won't go into the room and turn on the light, so to speak: it will be too painful to even look around.

Give yourself permission to look at things—this gives your child an opportunity to look at things for himself, too. This permission to awaken is a gift to yourself to your child, and to the generations yet to come, one they will experience as a result of your bravery in participating in the 10 Keys process.

And finally, remember that nobody gets to be wrong here. In fact, what if we believed there is no *wrong*? How much more fun could we have living life large and taking chances to have it all and experience it all, without fearing failure and stifling our passion and creations?

Make the choice to believe that your choices are perfect. When you make a choice, ask yourself, *What's good about it? What about it is serving me? Do I want to continue that or do I want to make a change because it brings me even more joy?*

(and not because I'm bad-and-wrong for making the first choice that I made.)

C: Compassion for Self

C is for *Compassion*, which is not compassion in a biblical sense, nor is it compassion for everyone else, which is the way most of us live our lives. The compassion I'm talking about is compassion for yourself first. Give yourself a break. Let yourself off the proverbial hook. Forgive yourself for being right where you are at this moment in time.

As a parent: Put yourself first, put your relationship with your partner second. Then you will still have a lot left over for your children. Then you come to your children and teach them how to do the same thing. You model and mentor, instead of coming to your child as a depleted "I have given my life for you" shell.

Your child: Teach your child how to have compassion for herself, how to know what she wants, needs, and feels. Teach them how to think and question for themselves.

Compassion for your child is being able to hold space so you can listen to what the child is going through, without trying to fix it. Ask the child questions: what are you going to learn from this, how does it make you feel, what could you give yourself internally that would fill you up right now, what could be perfect about this situation, how does this change who you are to other people?

The challenge is to ask these questions with no attachment to their answer—no leading the witness—or they will sniff you out and refuse to be walked into a corner by their judge and jury.

Instead, your job is to remind them of their leadership, their own skills, their own self-sovereignty.

You can even announce to your child that you're about to try something new: For example, Mom might say to the child: *"Normally, I would dive right in and separate you two"*…. but this time, I'm going to do something different."

1. Check in with yourself…*how am I feeling…do I need a time-out before I respond*?

2. How do you feel? (Each child gets an uninterrupted turn.)

3. What do you want to tell the other person?

4. How did you contribute to the argument/situation/issue? Your sister is crying right now…what if you took responsibility for that? What would you do differently right now? If you're crying, what if you took responsibility for that? What would you do differently right now?

5. What are you learning from this right now?

6. What can you say that will make you feel like you have your power back?

7. How do you want this situation to happen differently next time, if there is a next time?

8. What would you like the outcome to be?

Do you want to be playing together, would you like private time, nap, hungry, one-on-one time with mom?

At all times, resist the impulse to say the words you know they want to hear, make them feel better, be the superhero that fixes everything...the goal is not for you to be right and in your own Inner 7 Year Old know-it-all. The goal for you is to step aside and empower your children to think, to be aware of their own reactions, intentions, and what they're creating in their lives, to make new choices, and take responsibility for their behavior and, ultimately, their results.

A parent admitted to me that this being right, being the superhero, is the one great best thing about being a parent. It means you're always right! But do your best to put this aside. Visually give yourself all you need, internally, so you don't have to take the superhero drug.

With these questions, the role of the parent becomes that of detective, with the goal being that the children start thinking like the detectives, and figure out their own upset and their own new choices and new creations of what's next.

Be compassionate for what is, right now, in this moment. Be at peace with what is, right now, in this moment. If you're up for a stretch-goal, figure out what's perfect about what is in this moment, and be willing to consider that you are the creator of what *is* in this moment.

If you take the ownership for being the creator of what is, then you have the power to create something new. And that leads us to our next Key...*Own Your Story*.

O: Own Your Story

The second key is *Own Your Story*. To do this, you must first make absolutely sure you undertake Key One with tons of love and compassion for what currently is in this moment. Without Compassion, this key will feel like one big two-by-four to hit yourself over the head with and a means to blame yourself for your current lot in life. Only when you are ready to fully embrace Compassion, do you want to embark on the next most exciting journey to find out what your current story is.

How?, you might ask. If you really are ready to know what your current story is, look around you. See what you have interpreted in your life. That's your story.

So if you think you are broke, your story is you're broke. If you think you are fat, your story is you're fat. If you think you're unhappy, your story is you're unhappy. If you're a millionaire, your story has been you're a millionaire. So look at your story and use these 10 Keys to help you create that life.

I often see people manipulate a situation so they will fail on their own terms, rather than trying at something, playing the hand, and seeing how it turns out. *The world's not safe, good guys can't win, life isn't fair, a man will always disappoint you,* etc. These stereotypes, these stories, are what we live into, *unless we own our story*. Own the story, and you own the outcome, as well.

As a parent: There is no such thing as a "good" child, a "perfect" child, a "wonderful" child, and a "horrible, terrible" parent. Conversely, there is no such thing as a "perfect" parent who has an "awful" child.

If I, as a parent, believe that my child is bad, then my child most likely will believe me. If I, as a parent, believe that I am a good parent, then my child has nothing but good to live into, as well.

So what are you going to choose to believe? You

will look for evidence, no matter what the story, and I promise you will find it. Be careful what you choose to live into. Are you willing to be wrong about that past story that is not working for you, and are you ready to live into a more productive, fun, powerful, compassionate story?

Your child: If the child says, "I'm stupid," "I don't have any friends," or "Nobody loves me," they are looking for proof of their story...and they get to be right. You could ask your child:

1. Where do you want to go with this? Where do you want to be with this?

2. Are you looking to move through these feelings? What's your intention?

3. Tell me more. Let the child talk it out.

For that teenager who is an a "my-life-sucks" spiral, I would tell them to feel your feelings, name them, write them down, yell them out, cry them out, turn UP the volume, give yourself permission to stay in that space without making yourself bad-and-wrong, and when you're ready to move through it, then use *Own Your Story*.

Once the child is ready to use *Own Your Story*, ask them:

1. What does it mean to you? What story are you making up about this incident? Why do you think that happened? What are you making it mean?

2. Can you make up five reasons about why that happened? (These will usually be negative stories.)

3. Can you make up five more positive reasons about why that happened? (These can be wild and crazy, fun and silly. You might have to help by getting it started) Like—you get to be right and make them WRONG!!! You get to feel superior. You get to feel in-control. You get to blame someone else for your current feelings.

4. How do you feel when you believe the negative stories? How do you feel when you believe the positive stories? What if all the stories we just created were all made up? Which one do you choose to believe? If negative stories make you feel bad and positive stories make you feel good, then what do you choose to feel next?

5. What would you like to create instead?

Whatever your story is, you get to be right...so choose wisely and have fun with your conscious choices!

M: Mirror, Mirror

The third key is *Mirror, Mirror*.

First, a small, but serious, warning. Some of these concepts should not be used without Key One, which is *Compassion*. It's tremendously important to have compassion as you look at this key. *Mirror, Mirror* is meant to be used not necessarily in the heat of a hurtful moment, but later, afterward, when you're ready to move forward and potentially manifest change.

Mirror, Mirror is considering the possibility with playfulness and tons of compassion that if you are triggered, enraged, and feeling totally out of control, then maybe-just-maybe "as you spot it, you got it."

So if you think someone's stupid, you may be afraid of your own "inner stupid," which we all have at times when we can't see our own blind spots. Or if you think someone is absolutely beautiful and prettier than you, you might want to look again and find that beauty in you, as well.

This doesn't necessarily mean that if somebody is a child molester and you are enraged and totally triggered, that you're one, too, but it *might* mean that you're abusing your own inner child. You're defying and denying and not taking care of your own inner child, and thereby, hurting yourself.

This is not to mean that *Mirror, Mirror* is the "TRUTH" (which, you'll notice, is in quotation marks on purpose). *Mirror, Mirror* is a tool to use to transform highly emotionally-triggered moments of time. If I'm willing to look within at my own Stupid, or my own fill-in-the-blank judgment that I have about others, *then I might transform the outcome.*

Conversely, if you spot some positive characteristic in anybody else and it emotionally triggers or inspires you in any way—if you see someone and she is positively brilliant and it makes your heart sink—it might be because you're seeing *your* own untapped potential or own unacknowledged beauty.

If you see someone and you're on fire with who you think they are, it's because that possibility is within you. If you see someone and you're disgusted, and you're devastated, and you're furious, it's because you may be feeling that way about yourself.

Again, this tool is not the factual "TRUTH," it is only a powerful tool to be used to transform stuck judgments about others and to embrace some hidden gifts that you might not yet have seen, or have forgotten, within yourself.

As a parent:	*Mirror, Mirror* is a concept, a tool, to help you find your story. You do this by looking at yourself in the mirrors that are everywhere. That

reflection is not the truth, necessarily...it simply gives you a tool to look for clues for possible split-off, unconscious blind spots that you may not be aware of within yourself. If you're finding you're adamant that this is not you, if you're extremely triggered in the negative or significantly inspired by something in the positive, those are the aspects that if you look really closely, you will find those within yourself.

For example, if, as a mom, you can't stand your child's whining, needy constantly-complaining self, if you look really, really hard, you may find that part of yourself within, who has never gotten the chance to express *her* voice. You never got to feel needy, vulnerable, sad, so the child doing that triggers *you*.

Similarly, if you can't stand a little bad-ass, there might be a little teenager with you who wants to say all the politically incorrect things in your head, but if you're being politically correct and socially compliant, then so should everyone else. The more angry you are about it, the more difficult it is to bite your own tongue, because you're having difficulties with your own Inner Teen.

1. With compassion, give yourself permission to see it, feel it, name it, acknowledge it, whatever that trigger is.

2. Look for the gift that is concealed by the trigger.

3. Ask yourself: *Is there some part of me that's screaming to be heard because I'm in pain?*

4. Ask: *Is it something I'm doing to others that is hurtful or painful, and I want to*

change who I'm being to other people? (Hint: if this is something you're doing to others, you are quite likely to be doing it to yourself, as well.)

5. Ask: *Is this being done to me because I'm allowing it, and do I need to set some boundaries on not allowing this to happen further?*

Your child:

If I called you a pink-polka-dotted elephant, would you care? Then why do you care if people call you a geek or a loser?

You only get triggered if there is some part of the names that you believe. See if you can find the truth in it, find what part of you believes that behavior, that comment, or that thought is real.

Can you find the geek and loser in you? Can you be at peace with that judgment? If not, you will become extremely upset any time someone says those words to you, and you will give that person ALL your power.

The way to take your power back is to fall in love with whatever the person is saying. You could tell yourself it is their story, not yours—very similar to sticks and stones will break my bones, but words can never hurt me— *unless I believe those words are true and think I am bad-and-wrong because of it.*

1. Feel your feelings, name them out, give yourself permission to hurt...until you're ready not to.

2. Then, ask yourself: what did you hear them say that you are choosing to believe?

3. Do you believe those things are true? Can you live with yourself if it is true? Is it within your power to change something about yourself if you don't want it to be true? For example, if someone calls you a mean person, is there any truth in it? Do you want to transform your mean, or can you be okay with what you did and let that person think what they choose to think about you?

The positive aspect of *Mirror, Mirror* is this: when you see someone on the news, a singer, entertainer, who moves you, touches you, inspires you...that is also because there's a part of you that wants to come out and be seen the way you see that individual. Anything you see in them is within you.

Whatever your child sees in you that they admire, they will become. That's what they see in you, and that's what they want to become...if they believe they can. What a gift, if they could hear from you—*one of these days, you'll not only have what I have, but more.*

Children fear besting their parents. Give your child permission to be bigger and better and faster and stronger and have more money. Most parents say, "Of course, I want my children to be bigger, better, stronger, BEST than me." However, you may unconsciously feel that if your child reaches a new level, one that you think you did not and should have attained, then you may be thinking and unconsciously transmitting this to your child: *"If you (the child) are better than me, then I (the parent) have somehow failed."*

As the old story goes, the apple doesn't fall far from the tree. As a parent, if you haven't healed your patterns, your child will unconsciously live right into those patterns in order for both of you to heal. The child may consciously or unconsciously act out: *I do what you do, not what you say.* You may emotionally fear that your child will do what you did, whatever the thing is that you are still feeling guilt and shame about, and are still attempting to control the situation so that it does not happen to your child.

Consequently, your child feels controlled and rebels into the same behavior. After all, if the pattern was good enough for you (their hero), it is good enough for them.

An example of a way this apple/tree gets acted out is when a child is raised by a single parent, they can frequently become emotionally parentified...become the substitute spouse of the parent.

This is not conscious, of course, but because the parent is wounded and in pain and emotionally attached to shame and rage of the prior relationship, the child begins to attempt to meet the parent's emotional needs. When the parent subsequently finds a partner who can meet their emotional needs, then the child can feel like a jilted lover.

This can also happen with married couples, in which the child becomes the primary partner of one of the parents because that parent is not getting her or his needs met within the primary relationship. When the child considers finding his own partnership and getting his needs met within his existing relationship, it may not feel safe to leave the current, parentified relationship.

If any of that feels familiar or sounds familiar, remember that you are not bad-and-wrong.

P: Playful-Messy

The fourth key is Playful-Messy. This is one of my favorites. Playful-Messy is your reminder that life is both messy and fun.

If you can't have fun with life and if you aren't willing to make a mess, you might as well sit on the sidelines or hide under the covers. No matter what the game is, you'll always be in the cheap seats. The *safe* seats.

So Playful-Messy means that you are willing to put it out there, willing to play full-out, willing to make a mess, make mistakes.

In baseball, a great batting average is .400. A decent batting average in the major leagues is .350. This means that for every 10 times a player came up to the plate to bat, he got a hit only three or four times. Six or seven of those times, he struck out! You cannot hit a home run unless you are also willing to strike out, many, many times.

Edison, one of our nation's treasures, worked for years to invent the light bulb. If he invented the light bulb on his one-thousandth try, that means he also knows 999 ways NOT to invent a light bulb!

How many times in your life have you ever tried to do something 999 times and been willing to fail, to fall on your face?

But I'm not Edison, goes the thought in your head.

Okay, about you: if you are walking today, it is because you were willing to fall down, over and over again, as a toddler.

So my question to you is, can you imagine when you were six months or a year old and you said: "That's it. I've fallen on my face one too many times." Or, "I've gone potty in my diapers for the last time. I'm quitting. I will never be potty-trained, and I will never walk again." The key is to stay in that place where we can see those life lessons as playful and messy, rather than failures or humiliations. Have fun, and make a mess!

As a parent: You've no doubt heard the expression "you should make peace with failure." What if there was no such thing as failure? There are just learning experiences. This approach takes the sting out of the seven-year-old shame and seriousness of not getting something "RIGHT" the first time we attempt a new experience. We then get to make choices based on what will bring us pleasure, rather than avoiding that which we fear, or what we're taught to avoid.

The way you teach your child that it's okay to fail is by modeling failure gracefully.

Your child: I tell children: don't be afraid to try again. It's not supposed to be perfect. Life is exploration...if you're not making a mess, you're playing too small. If you're not failing, then you haven't graduated to the next grade.

Would you rather be an expert first-grader at age 9, 14, 22, or would you rather be a second-grader and be a little bit out of your depth? You get to learn all these new concepts...it's about learning, not about perfection.

If I'm never willing to be a beginner, I'll never learn how to ski, dance, drive a car, type, paint, be a carpenter, a singer, etc. I invite everyone to be a beginner at something at every stage of your life. You have to be willing to start from scratch. Who's willing to be playful and make a MESS with perfection?

A: Affect

The fifth Key is *Affect*. *Affect* is another word for feelings. My theory is that the vast majority of addictions and chronic illnesses (ulcers, heart attack, high blood pressure) are caused by not being okay, safe, able, comfortable with feelings and understanding how to express one's affect.

Instead, we feel anxiety, overwhelmed, upset, stressed, so we numb ourselves with drugs, alcohol, shopping, sex, all the –*isms*. Until we have made peace with feelings, we will need tools to numb or deaden the affect to feel safe and back in our "happy" place.

Your body has the same physiological responses to excitement and anxiety. Your heart rate and respiration increase, you may have trouble breathing, etc. If you associate a negative meaning to those physiological feelings, then you will avoid doing anything that elicits those feelings in you. But if you enjoy those physiological feelings and associate a positive meaning to them, then you will seek situations that give rise to those feelings.

That's why some people love horror movies and roller coasters, and some love to watch those tearjerker movies that make them cry. The sensation, the physiological response, that accompanies these activities, is pleasurable, a positive association, and they go on that roller coaster again and again whenever given the (safe) opportunity.

That's why some enjoy running marathons or triathlons...these are the types of things we do to be able to experience those physical sensations on our terms, with a meaning we attach to those sensations. Others might think of running a marathon as abusive or sheer terror. What's your story?

As an exercise, you might want to identify a feeling and describe the situation without judgment.

I feel _____ when _____.

For example, you might first write:

I feel   (mad sad scared upset lonely
               tired hurt)
when you   don't have time to talk to me.

Now, if someone said that out loud to you, how would you feel? Like: I feel mad when you act like a self-centered, egotistical idiot.

If the "when you" part would hurt to hear, then try to revise it so that it is strictly descriptive, without being judgmental.

I feel	(mad sad scared upset lonely tired hurt)
when you	don't have time to talk to me before you go to bed.

Once you have the first two parts down, it's time to add on:

I feel	(mad sad scared upset lonely tired hurt)
when you	don't have time to talk to me before you go to bed
because	I tell myself you don't care about me.

What's your negative, made-up-story as to the "why" of the behavior?

Then add the part you want to change:

I feel	(mad sad scared upset lonely tired hurt)
when you	don't have time to talk to me before you go to bed
because	I tell myself you don't care about me
and I	would prefer/love it if we could have some quality time to connect and love each other before bedtime.

And if you feel you need to, add a consequence:

I feel	(mad sad scared upset lonely tired hurt)
when you	don't have time to talk to me before you go to bed

because and I	I tell myself you don't care about me would prefer/love it if we could have some quality time to connect and love each other before bedtime. And if you don't, I will have to... Or if you don't, I will choose to...

Remember that demands and threats are met with resistance (defiance!), while requests are usually at least considered. A request also means that you will be all right if the other person, for whatever reason, cannot meet your need in this area. Remember also that you can have a backup plan to meet your own needs.

To sum it up, the more demands you make, the more defiance you will generate in the lives of those around you, and the more anger and frustration you will have in your life.

A third, radical alternative is to listen to what might be causing your partner to go to bed without talking to you. Ask what they might be feeling angry or hurt about that is causing them to not feel safe or not want to be in a relationship with you.

Look within to see who you might be being that is living you into the results that you are experiencing and the stories that you are telling yourself.

If you ask your partner about his feelings, don't be surprised if he has a perfectly logical explanation that has absolutely nothing to do with you, like *I was reprimanded at work today and feeling really bad about myself, and I did not want to ruin your day.*

Your partner just lived you right into their story by not sharing their affect. Instead, he transformed it by expressing and getting love and support from you. He might have even had a beer to keep the feeling from even being expressed. It's interesting how we do this to each other all the time. Start looking for the patterns.

**As a
parent:**
You can feel your feelings, or you can unconsciously act them out on others or yourself. This is the classic example of hurting the ones you love, such as snapping at your kids because you're really upset about your controlling boss who humiliated you at the staff meeting.

And there's no cheating with *Affect*: you can't inhibit or suppress or depress one emotion, without inhibiting *all* emotions. When you inhibit yourself to keep from feeling anger, for example, you also restrict yourself from experiencing the full feeling of joy, happiness, or of love.

If you don't master the ability to experience full range of emotions, you also won't get the full experience of the "good" emotions.

**Your
child:**
Feelings are energy. They are not the truth. A feeling is not a fact.

Having a big feeling of being mad is not the same as hurting someone.

Feelings pass. If you give yourself permission to feel a feeling, then there are lots of things you can do with your feelings. If you're mad, you can hit a pillow, you can scream, you can yell, you can journal, you can shake it off...you have choices when it comes to experiencing an emotion. What is an okay way for your child to express emotions? Can you handle and hold their big feelings without going down with the proverbial punch?

A special note about children and the word *no*—
children are explorers. To a child, being told no is
like you placing a bite of delicious chocolate cake
on her tongue and being told not to swallow.

The less you force your children to do this, the
less angry they'll become.

S: Self-Care

Key number five is *Self-Care*. *Self-Care* is care on the
outside, taking care of your external body, and *Self-Care* on the
inner body, as well. Do the Inner Family visualization exercise in
the prior chapter. Meet the needs of your Inner Family. Give
your Inner 3 Year Old hugs and/or an inner ice cream bar. Give
your Inner 7 Year Old accolades and awards for all her wins and
successes. Give your Inner Teen an inner fan club, permission to
have her passionate authentic voice.

If I don't take care of myself, I become a burden to my
family and to society.

If I don't pay my bills, I become a burden to the state. If I
don't eat right, I'm going to have medical problems down the
line, and somebody's going to have to pay those bills.

If I don't take care of myself, then my child *is not safe*.

If I don't take care of myself, then I'm more likely to
resent and be angry at my child.

And the child learns from you that Self-Care isn't
important and doesn't need to be done. You are teaching your
child how *not* to take care of themselves: *I do what you do, not
what you say*. Words are cheap, they think!! If it's not necessary
for you, why would you think I should do it, as well?

What they tell you on the airplane is right: put your own
mask on first.

When you take care of yourself first, you will be there to
show up and bring energy to the relationship. When you make
your partnership a priority second, you will continue to have a

partner and help raising your child together. And then you will both be there to take care of and raise your children, third.

Moms, in particular, need permission to take care of themselves. They don't take care of themselves, and then their children end up needing to take care of them—the parentified adult I talked about earlier! This becomes a negative inter-generational pattern to address.

When you "put the child first," you are being a martyr, a saint, a super-duper 7-year-old. You're doing that martyr-saint thing like you'll get a payoff. I'll give and give and give, until someday, when my kids will pay me back. Well, the thing is, they can never catch up to that and will never be able to pay back that debt. They will feel shameful and overwhelmed for hurting the one they adore, and feel bad about themselves for taking so much from you—all as a result of YOUR, choice, not theirs!

If I put chocolate on your tongue, would you swallow? It's so hard to put the boundaries on yourself. So let me give you an example. Does your child ever say:

> *Mom, please don't take me to see my best friend when you are depleted and exhausted, please don't give me all those great toys that you and I both know are out of your budget, please don't cook me my favorite food or clean up after me while the clothes are being washed and you are working your second job. Please sit down, take a load off. You deserve a foot rub.*

If your child does do this, they are becoming a parentified adult. They are learning to take care of *you* because you don't take care of yourself.

Self-Care is both an art of awareness and an exercise in creativity. If the only thing that will meet my needs is to take a trip to Paris, then I will be miserable until that need is met. But if I can find a way to meet that need, say, by bringing Paris into my bedroom and my car and my office space, and eating French food, then maybe I can satisfy the need that Paris represents (maybe it represents freedom or escape). I find creative ways to give Paris to myself, instead of being furious that I can't afford to go.

As a parent:

As I mentioned earlier, when I ask children: *Would you rather tell your parent no and get to be frustrated or disappointed, or would you rather they tell you yes, and they get to be the one who is frustrated and disappointed?*

100% of the time, kids tell me they would rather be told *no* and be the frustrated-disappointed one, than carry the burden of their parents' shame or anger.

Most of the time, they want to ask for (whatever), they want you and expect you to say no, and they want to feel their feelings when you do say no. They want to share those feelings with you.

This same concept works for your Inner Child, as well. If having that donut feels good in the moment, but later on you're going to beat yourself up and make yourself bad-and-wrong, then that's not *Self-Care*, that's torture. It's like putting chocolate on your own tongue and telling you not to swallow, or beating yourself up for enjoying the bite. If getting a mani-pedi and a massage feels good in the moment, but later, you feel like a horrible parent for taking the time or spending the money, then that's torture, too.

As a parent: For it to be *Self-Care*, each member of your Inner Family must be in alignment, agreement, on the choice, and within budget so that everyone feels safe.

If you're not sure a particular choice will be *Self-Care*, ask yourself:

Is it what my body wants and needs?
Is it what my emotional soul wants and needs?
Is it what my psyche wants and needs?
Is it what my Inner 3 Year Old needs?
Is it what my Inner 7 Year Old needs?
Is it what my Inner Teen needs?

If the answers to these questions are all yes, then you're doing *Self-Care*. If any of these answers is no, then you may be moving yourself into a situation where you might later feel like making yourself bad-and-wrong.

Your child: You get to be dependent as long as you choose to depend on someone else to meet your needs (and as long as they are willing to take care and enable those needs). When you want self-sovereignty and freedom, when you want to have control over your destiny, then you must also be 100% accountable and responsible for your consequences.

If you want to get whatever grades you want to get, then you must be prepared to pay the increase in the auto insurance payment. When you make the money, you get to determine the upper limit on what gets ordered during a family dinner at a restaurant.

You may find you have too much dependence on other people, that you have the need to make other people happy.

For example, if someone says something nasty on the playground, you have choices: you can avoid that person, you can ask for help from a third party, or you can choose to ignore what the person says and make up a new story about what it might even mean about that person—they didn't get enough loving in their childhood.

Similarly, if you really want that bicycle (or skateboard or iPod) and your parents can't afford to buy it for you (and have set loving, clear, compassionate boundaries), you have options. You can buy a used one, you can get a job to earn the money for it, or you can put that material desire aside until it is a better financial time in you and your family's life.

S: Self-Trust

The sixth key is *Self-Trust*. This key is to Self-Trust externally, the principle of being your word, but also to Self-Trust internally, to know and trust that you are your own best friend, ally, mentor, leader, partner, etc., *to yourself*.

No one will ever believe in you the way that *you can* believe in you. With this key, wherever you go through life, you'll always have a friend, one you can count on. Wherever you go—there you are!!

Self-Trust is an underutilized art: the concept of re-learning what you want and need.

How many times have you had this conversation with your kid—or yourself?

Child says to Mom:	Mom says back:
I'm hungry!	You can't be hungry, you just ate!
I'm sleepy!	You can't be sleepy, you just had a nap!

It's not just the kids, either. We are no longer in touch with our internal monitors, with those parts that tell us the truth of how we're feeling. We've lost connection to our bodies. We all do it. The solution is to re-learn how to listen to ourselves.

As a parent: You're about to become the parent you always wish you had.

The down side is that you have to let go of the fantasy that someone's going to come in on a white horse and save you, that you've given and given and given and someone else is eventually, someday, going to ride up and give back to you.

The good news is that you can still have the perfect childhood or happiness without the white horse or anyone on it.

What if we can be our own best friend?

Self-Trust is talking and listening to ourselves, intuitively caring about what we want and need and feel, even if it seems no one else gives a darn about us and our needs.

Try setting an alarm, several times a day, to do an internal check-in. When the alarm goes off, ask your Inner 3 Year Old, "How are you doing? What do you want?" Then ask the same question of your Inner 7 Year Old and your Inner Teen.

And whatever answers you get back, *give that to yourself!*

Know also that if you tell yourself you want something and then you don't give it to yourself, you learn that you can't trust yourself. So set yourself up to win: ask yourself what it is you want, and find a way to give that to yourself. Give yourself kudos for figuring out what you want and satisfying those wants and needs. If you can't give it to yourself externally—you can ALWAYS find a way to give it to yourself internally.

Your child: We are not taught to think for ourselves and feel for ourselves. We are told what we are supposed to think and feel. When nobody knows how to think and feel, there is no *Self-Trust*.

We overeat and overspend, so we don't trust ourselves. In order to stop doing these habits, we need to re-learn what a normal amount of food is, and then learn our own, new feeling of "full." Even if you're not full, you wait until 20 minutes later and check in again.

That can work for an adult...but what if your teen doesn't have the patience or logic quite yet to wait the 20 minutes?

Then, you might have an open discussion about what might happen to their bodies if they ate anything they wanted, any time they wanted. Children have an amazing ability to reason it out, to express themselves, if you are really not attached to their outcome.

They know they don't want to end up weighing 500 pounds; they know they don't want to put that kind of strain on their bodies. In this way, through gentle questioning, you teach your child how to think this new way for themselves—what a foreign concept!

Ask the child what they want, what they need, and help them figure it out for themselves, even how to meet their own needs. Now, you might be in the equation, but you won't be the only answer to every question. This process can be frustrating; it can also be frustrating not to know. So you can say something like: *If I tell you what I think it is, that will be frustrating for you, too. So let's figure it out together.*

Try to redirect the questions so the child really is figuring it out for herself. Help them become their own investigators, detectives, so they can figure out their own wants, needs, desires, decisions, and choices.

After all, you can't satisfy a need or fulfill a want if you don't know what it is.

People die, people leave, people go away. You are the only one you can truly depend upon. Learn to depend on yourself first. Go within and make friends with and fall in love with your inner self. Anything you receive from everyone else will be icing on the cake, and best of all, you won't fear losing the icing because you will always have the cake—YOU!!

I: Intrinsic/Extrinsic Focus

Key Seven is *Intrinsic versus Extrinsic Focus*. There are at least two ways you can play this game. You can focus on the external to create your internal feelings, or you can focus on the internal feelings and visualizations to create your external manifestations.

As you focus externally on what you want, notice the wins, appreciate what already *is* externally, you will feel positive feelings by noticing and naming externally your gratitudes and blessings. If you focus on what you don't have and what is not working in your life, my educated guess is that you will feel miserable, upset, and won't feel like getting off the couch to do anything whatsoever that might be productive.

You can also use intrinsic focus to create external rewards, creations, and accomplishments. What you perceive on the inside, you manifest on the outside. What you believe on the inside will be the creation on the outside.

If I focus internally on what I love and appreciate about myself, flood my imagination with the feeling of how I feel "now" that I have my million dollars in the bank, now that I'm living with the partner of my dreams, now sporting the healthy, sexy body that even I envy, and anything else I might want to live into, with the most vivid visualizations and emotional ramifications I can muster.... After that visualization, do you think I will be more inclined to go for a walk, make those sales calls, go out on a blind date, etc.?

For this key, you need a lot of compassion, and a lot of playfulness. The idea is not to judge your current situation and make yourself bad-and-wrong. Without playfulness and creativity, you'll limit your transformation and possible opportunities.

First, some definitions: *intrinsic*. This is your internal focus. For example, you can live as a monk with a fantasy of bliss and harmony. Someone else feeds and clothes you; you don't have to worry about anything. That's total intrinsic.

Then, *extrinsic*, your external focus. For example, you can live in the external world where you are totally at the mercy of the attitudes of those around you—whether you're invited to a party or not, when your boss is in a bad mood, whether your kids talk back or not, whether or not your husband helps cheerfully with the housework. In this way, if things are good around you, you're good; if they're bad, then your life is bad. You get to blame everyone else for any unhappiness, which can be appealing and even a great high, but ultimately you're like a yo-yo, at the mercy of others.

In an ideal world, you'd have a perfect balance of both intrinsic and extrinsic focus, 100% of the time—not, as you might assume, a 50-50% split. Ideally, I'm 100% present to my external environment, while at the same time, I'm 100% present to my internal world, as well.

With this approach, I can have it all. Everything.

What if, by who I'm being, I can impact other people? You've heard this one before: if you have a bad attitude, a chip on your shoulder, negative energy, then you manifest that attitude around yourself. In all the bad situations that are happening to you, the common denominator is *you*, walking around with all that bad attitude.

But here's the thing...when I walk around like a victim like that, the world is a scary place, and blaming others helps keep me safe, makes me feel safe in the world.

If I can figure out a way to put the blame aside, to stop feeling like a victim, then I can assert control over the things that happen to me. The way I do that is to *take responsibility without taking blame*. (You can see how this Key, *Intrinsic/Extrinsic*, can be like walking on a tightrope!)

Another way to think about it is that we all make choices that, consciously or unconsciously, impact our lives.

For example, if I'm hit by a drunk driver, I can feel like a victim, like the drunk is 100% to blame. Or I can choose to view it as though I contributed to the situation; after all, I stayed at work till 1 a.m. and was tired driving home.

A caveat: *Intrinsic/Extrinsic* is not meant to be a 24x7 experience. Sometimes, you'll want to feel those feelings, wallow in that crappy day, live in the bad mood. And that's fine. (That's what Key Five, *Affect*, is all about.) But when you're ready to look at your situation differently, when you're ready to take control, when you are ready to get back in your power, when you're feeling compassionate with yourself, *that's* the time to take a look at *Intrinsic/Extrinsic*.

As a parent:	Remember all that advice...act like you're having a great time, catch more flies with sugar, how your parents tried to drill it into you, and the good advice is sometimes so hard to take? Well, there is a benefit to following this good advice: this is a good way to get your power back.
	When you act like you're having a great time, you do have the power in that moment.
Your child:	Play it like a game. *How would it be different if...*
	Teach your child how to visualize the intended outcome and flood himself with positive emotions during the process. Many Olympic athletes swear by this process. Many millionaires have a vision board, a goal setting chart, measurement, and monitoring to notice the road signs and celebrate all the way to the bank.
	Are you willing to be wrong about anything and everything you may have tried in the past in order to have it all?

One day, I did an experiment—I visualized and flooded myself with negative emotions (my normal, anxious-worry thoughts) and then observed what unfolded throughout the day. I tried just to be an observer in the experiment. The results were negative and typical proof of my negative story.

The next day, I visualized myself in all my power, as a licensed clinical psychologist, a keynote speaker, a singer/songwriter, loving life, having fun, and fully experiencing my wildest dreams, both visually and emotionally. I then observed the results and ramifications of my internal positive focus.

After alternating three days of each, the negative and positive days, I stopped the experiment on the next day.

Why? I was supposed to focus on the negative.

I thought to myself: this is crazy, it can't really be this simple. It cannot be that if I focus on negative, I find, see, feel, and experience negative results, and when I focus on positive, I find, see, feel, and experience positive results. I was not willing to try even one more day of the negative.

Why not try this experiment yourself? The rewards will be endless....

O: Organize Your Village

The eighth key is to organize your village, again intrinsically and extrinsically.

Organize your external village, then organize your internal village. Help your child learn the concept of even having an internal village and help them with the concept of setting up an external village.

To your child, *you* are their village—you, your spouse or partner, and maybe grandparents or a caregiver—that's their entire village.

So if mom's not available, the child is out of luck.

As a parent, it's your job to help your child identify his needs, so you can help him set up his personalized support team.

Ask your child, "What does your Inner 3 Year Old need?" If the answer is "more snuggles," where can you go in my external village to get that? Maybe I can ask my spouse to hold me. Or, if he's busy or away on a business trip, I can give that to myself, or buy a massage chair that gives me that same sensation of snuggling!

Ask yourself, "What does my Inner 7 Year Old need?" If the answer is, "I want to know that I'm a good mom," where can you go in my external village to get that need met? Who do you need to have around you so you can feel like a good mom?

For example, let's say you don't get enough date nights (as in never) with your spouse or partner. If you're like most couples, finding a babysitter you trust and can afford is an ongoing, never-ending task. If you're like most couples, it's easier and cheaper to stay home.

What if, instead, you approached two or three other couples, who are most likely also experiencing this particular issue, and asked if they wanted to set up a babysitting co-op? One couple would take the other couples' kids for a night, allowing the other co-op parents to go out and enjoy a date night. Then the next week, it would be that couple's turn to host the kids, and so on.

How would your home life improve if you had more stress-free, dedicated time with your spouse, and your kids had the independence- and skill-building time playing with other friendly families in your village?

Another idea is to have a family co-op. Everyone works together to meet one member-family's immediate project needs, such as cleaning out the basement, getting the yard work done, or painting a room. Everyone in the co-op gives up two hours a week, and the recipient has, say, ten willing people to help them get a job done. And this is great, but the best part is that these kinds of co-operative situations teach your children how to create community.

Building our external village seems like a bottom priority in most of our lives. I am going to assert that if it became a top priority for us, and we built our external village to support us, it would be so much easier for us to handle all the other competing priorities.

But I hear you asking, *how*?

The way you create the internal village is to go intrinsic-to-extrinsic. For example, if your Inner 3 Year Old wants an ice cream bar, then visualize, internally, giving her that ice cream bar. If your Inner 7 Year Old wants organization and a team of experts at her beck and call, visualize that internally on her behalf. Imagine your Inner 7 Year Old as the center, the heartbeat, of her own home-based business, if that's what she wants.

Whatever your Inner Family desires, if you visualize it internally, it manifests externally.

Now here is the paradox: the "negative" things we experience, such as wanting to eat an entire tub of ice cream in one sitting, we visualize internally in order to keep ourselves from having them manifest externally. By contrast, the "good" things, such as becoming a leader in our profession, we visualize internally so that it will manifest externally.

As a parent:	Set time with yourself to check in with the young, inner parts of yourself. If you routinely check in with your Inner 3 Year Old, Inner 7 Year Old, and Inner Teen, and visualize internally meeting their needs, whatever they are, you are less likely to act those needs out externally.
Your child:	Ask your child these same types of questions. Even if your child is not by nature an outgoing, socially comfortable child, these types of questions, over time, will help her become more socially comfortable.

N: kNOw Your Boundaries

Know your boundaries. I can't say *yes* without an option to say *no*. And it is absolutely essential that I am able to say no, or no one will be able to trust my *yes*—including me!

Has this ever happened to you? I ask someone who works with me, "Will you be in the office at 8 o' clock?" And they say:

"Sure, sure, sure." The next day they are not there until 9 o'clock, because they said *yes*, but their teenager says *no*.

Someone says, "I'll get you that project. No problem, I'll get that to you in two days." Your Inner 7 Year Old said, "Sure, I'll get that handled." Your inner teenager said, "You and what army?"

Notice in these two examples how it's the Inner Teen who always gets in the way?

So know your boundaries, know your desires, ask your Inner Teenager what she's willing to do and what she's willing not to do. What are your internal boundaries?

An internal boundary would be: it's just absolutely not okay to beat myself up. It's not okay to make myself bad-and-wrong. So the second I catch myself beating myself up, I give myself permission to be okay with *what is*.

Another internal boundary is to create rules that work for me, so that I get to win. For example, I used to have a to-do list that was 100 items long. I would get tons of stuff done, but my list was so long and overwhelming that I was always feeling like I'd failed. Now, having set my internal boundary, I have about seven things on my to-do list. The way I tell my Inner 7 Year Old that I get to win is to accomplish one, two, or three, depending on the scope.

The interesting thing is that now the vast majority of days—actually, I can't even think of a day in the distant past that I have not won. And generally speaking, I can always get all seven things done. I always set it up so that I get to feel like a HUGE Winner! My rules, my boundaries, my manifestations of my results, and best of all, my celebrations.

As a parent: Know your internal boundaries, as well as your external boundaries.

The challenge with owning your boundary is controlling yourself, not controlling the people around you. If my boundary is about controlling you, then I'm going to be very frustrated and unhappy. If my boundary is about controlling me, then I have a much better chance of getting my needs met.

Your child: If you're on the playground, some other kids are yelling at you and that's a boundary for you, how can you resolve that situation? If you try to control your friends and keep them from yelling, how does that work for you? Can you make someone else stop yelling? No? So what's another alternative that you can do to stop getting yelled at? Wear earplugs, tell a teacher, just smile and forget it, play on another part of the playground, tell the other person how it makes you feel...there are lots to control yourself.

Signs of unhealthy boundaries:
Check all that you think describe you

☐ Trusting no one—trusting anyone—black and white thinking
☐ Tell all
☐ Talking at intimate level on first meeting
☐ Falling in love with new acquaintance
☐ Falling in love with anyone who reaches out
☐ Being overwhelmed by a person—preoccupied
☐ Acting on first sexual impulse
☐ Being sexual for partner, not self
☐ Going against personal values or rights to please others
☐ Not noticing when someone else displays inappropriate boundaries
☐ Not noticing when someone invades your boundaries
☐ Accepting food, gifts, touch, sex that you don't want
☐ Touching a person without asking
☐ Taking as much as you can get for the sake of getting
☐ Giving as much as you can give for the sake of giving
☐ Allowing someone to take as much as they can from you
☐ Letting others direct your life
☐ Letting others describe your reality
☐ Letting others define you
☐ Believing others can anticipate your needs
☐ Expecting others to fill your needs automatically
☐ Falling apart so someone will take care of you
☐ Self abuse: food, work, alcohol, drugs, etc.
☐ Sexual and physical abuse

Signs of Healthy Boundaries:
Check all that you think describe you

- ❑ Appropriate trust
- ❑ Revealing a little of yourself at a time, then checking to see how the other person responds
- ❑ Moving step by step into intimacy
- ❑ Putting a new acquaintanceship on hold until you check for compatibility
- ❑ Deciding whether a potential relationship will be good for you
- ❑ Staying focused on your own growth and recovery
- ❑ Weighing the consequence before acting on sexual impulse
- ❑ Being sexual when you want to be sexual—concentrating largely on your own pleasure, rather than monitoring reactions of partner
- ❑ Maintaining personal values despite what others want
- ❑ Noticing when someone else displays inappropriate boundaries
- ❑ Noticing when someone invades your boundaries
- ❑ Saying "no" to food, gifts, touch, sex you don't want
- ❑ Asking a person before touching them
- ❑ Respect for others—not taking advantage of someone's generosity
- ❑ Self-respect—not giving too much in hope that someone will like you
- ❑ Not allowing someone to take advantage of your generosity
- ❑ Trusting your own decisions
- ❑ Defining your truth, as you see it
- ❑ Knowing who you are and what you want
- ❑ Recognizing that friend and partners are not mind-readers
- ❑ Clearly communicating your wants and needs (and recognizing that you may be turned down, but you can ask)
- ❑ Becoming your own loving parent
- ❑ Talking to yourself with gentleness, humor, love, and respect

External and Internal Boundaries:

Purpose: Protection, Identification
1. Keep people from invading my emotional and physical space
2. Keep me from invading others' space
3. Help me identify "me"
4. Safety for self and others

External Boundaries Help Me:
1. Choose my own distance
2. Control touching, physical, sexual interactions
3. Protect my physical space

Internal Boundaries Help:
1. Protect our thinking, feeling and behavior
2. Take responsibility for thinking, feelings, and behavior and keeps them separate from others. Stop blaming others for mine.
3. Stop us from taking responsibility for other's thoughts, feelings, and behaviors.
4. Stop us from controlling and manipulating others.

Healthy:
- Boundaries that are permeable at my discretion. I am empowered to protect myself. I respect my boundaries and others.

Unhealthy:
- No boundaries: transgress others, subtle or abusive. (Very small children have no boundaries. They learn them by the way they are treated, respected.)
- None: Trouble saying "no," taking space, no sense of being abused or abusing, let others take advantage of them, lack protection, trouble with other's need for boundaries, feels rejected.
- Confused: Set them, withdraw them, varies according to whom, and takes responsibility for others.

- Walls: Usually of fear or anger, withdrawal or words. Used to retreat or frighten off. Wall of fear not effective protection.
- Conflicted: Walls—none—walls—none—walls. Risks, usually unwisely, vulnerability = pain, fear retreats behind walls = lonely.

We learn our sense of boundaries from our relationship with our parents.

How do the 10 Keys Relate to Life?

These 10 Keys relate to every single solitary aspect of life. I've started with parenting, 10 Keys to Compassionate Parenting, but the secret is that even if you are happily childless, you will learn parenting skills so that you can parent your own Inner Family. If you come as a parent for the sake of your children, you will find so many tools to integrate with your spouse, to integrate with your boss, your health, your wealth, your environment, the world, and in business. I apply these 10 Key concepts to every single facet of my life.

What Benefits do the 10 Keys Offer Parents?

So this 10 Keys process, this 10 Keys program, when taken, will help your children become their own life leaders. They will find their own Divine Wise Selves as you find your Divine Wise Self. As you de-clutter, they will de-clutter.

A mother that I was working with has been dealing with clutter for six, seven years. Her *Mirror, Mirror* story was that she always makes a mess, her life is a mess and she has clutter everywhere. Well, one day, she mastered it. She completely cleaned up her office. Everything that had been cluttered was completely cleaned up.

Five minutes later, her daughter, twelve years old at the time, came in with eight bags of clothes, and said: "Mom, I want to give these clothes to Goodwill."

The mother was in shock. She hadn't even told her daughter that she was doing the de-cluttering.

So as a parent, when you implement these 10 Keys, de-clutter, your children will de-clutter. You break old patterns, and your children break the same patterns, but at much younger ages. You live your dreams, and your children instantly see the possibility of following your footsteps, and they figure this all out at a young age.

I mentioned one of my favorite stories earlier, about the musician who had five children, and all of them are phenomenal musicians. As he decided to take the risk and record, *all five* of his children followed him into the recording studio to start their public musical careers.

The apple doesn't fall far from the tree. This is a fact; I see this happen all the time with parents and children. I could go into bars, hear stories, and win bets on what happened to peoples' parents, grandparents, and great-grandparents...and predict what's going to happen to their children if they continue to believe and do what's on their current life path.

If you got pregnant when you were 16, the chances and the odds are 101 percent that your child will follow in your footsteps, unless either:

- you fall in love and make peace with it, or
- your child falls in love and makes peace with it and understands and learns life lessons from it.

So for anything in your life you don't want your child to model—money, health, wealth, business, relationships—you need the 10 Keys to Compassion.

With the 10 Keys to Compassion, you can learn to be at peace with these issues and thereby avoid their pitfalls and the pain and suffering that ensues.

How do the 10 Keys Impact Teenagers?

In my seminar experiences, teens get this material 50 times faster than the parents. If I have a group of 15 teens going through this process, I can do it in half the time that it would take me to do the work with their parents, and the teens will implement the new behaviors and come back and see me again.

This is because they are open, they are not stuck in a story, they are not invested in being right about their life-long patterns and their life-long beliefs.

I had a 16-year-old in one of my classes. At the end of the two-hour course, she was in tears. "Why am I just now learning this?" she asked me. She couldn't believe that she was 16 and no one had told her these concepts. As it happens, there was a 60-year-old woman in the same class, and she said she could relate. No one had ever told her those concepts, either.

These concepts need to be told and taught to children, starting at the youngest of ages, so children become empowered, they become responsible, and they get that it's their life and their responsibility, that they can be held accountable to consciously create their life, any day, in any way they choose to create it.

4. 10 Keys in Action

The 10 Keys Process

Once you're in your filled-up, feel-good space, dealing with your children positively comes naturally and instinctively.

So we use the 10 Keys to get ourselves back in our power, get ourselves back to feeling good, find our inner voice, and prepare ourselves to help and guide our children to do the same.

In general, whenever a parent asks me a question, what I'm looking for first is "what does the mom need in that moment to be ready and willing and able to hear the child?" Is the mom angry, tired, or depleted? Is she in her Inner 3 Year Old, or her Inner 7 Year Old workaholic, or is she in her Inner Teen, just sick of the Inner 7 Year Old rat race?

So, first we need to address mom's issues. The mom knows what to give herself once she is back in her power, so do your best to connect with your Divine Wise Self. Many times, what mom needs is just to vent (that's the teenager needing to be heard). Maybe the mom's Inner 7 Year Old needs to be acknowledged for all her hard work, for all the good she's doing. Maybe her Inner 3 Year Old needs to be held and given permission to feel, acknowledge that she is safe, that her kids are safe, that she's normal, that she's not the only one to feel these big, huge, crazy feelings. Her Inner 3 Year Old needs hope: this, too, shall pass, we'll get to the other side, you are not alone, and you are not crazy.

Ask your Inner 3 Year Old these questions:

How am I doing physically? How am I doing emotionally? Is my body tired? Is my body hungry? Am I feeling a sugar-low? Am I having a food allergy, such as a gluten allergy, that can be kicking in right now? Am I feeling hormonal? Is my body safe? Am I feeling sad? Am I feeling scared? Am I feeling vulnerable? If all of those things are okay, *am I feeling bad-and-wrong?*

If I'm feeling bad-and-wrong, it's most likely due to an issue my Inner 7 Year Old is having.

Ask your Inner 7 Year Old these questions:

Do I feel like I can't get it right? Do I feel like I can't win? Do I feel like I haven't done enough? Do I feel like I don't know what the rules are? Do I feel like no matter what I do, it is never enough? Do I feel like I have failed? Do I feel like I should have done more, completed more, be further along?

In order to counter some of these feelings, you can do a Brag List of all the great stuff you've done recently, or if you have a severely active inner dialogue, you might need to go back to childhood—I did.

See if you can write down 100-plus accomplishments, success stories, brags about your life. The more lenient and generous you are with yourself, the more giving and gracious your children will be with themselves, and with you. If you are stingy with your wins, they will be stingy with their compliments, as well.

I double-dog dare you to give yourself permission to feel the good feeling of being a winner—how good can you stand it? There is no wrong way to do this exercise. This is a fantastic exercise to do around the dinner table, if everyone knows and abides by the rules.

This is an important one for both parents to talk about before the experience. For many of us, we were taught bragging is a bad thing. It is in doing this exercise, with those that you love and feel safe to share your success with, that you won't need to brag and exaggerate to strangers to get the love and be seen for who you are. Teach your children by allowing you and your spouse to play full-out. One critical concept of this game is to accept all brags that anyone shares as positive; demeaning, questioning or challenging another's success is an absolute way to kill the positive power of this process.

See www.drbeth.com/embracingdefiance for an expanded article and handouts how to play this game.

Another way to play this game and teach your children is to identify your current life rules.

The way to identify what your current rules are is to identify what you're mad or upset about and acknowledge the rule underneath it. For example, you might feel the kitchen's a mess and a good woman/wife/mother would have this all clean before she went to bed.

When you find that "should," that's the rule you've set up for yourself as a prerequisite to happiness. *Then* I get to relax. *Then* I get to have fun. *Then* I get to be happy. The best thing about identifying the rules is that You, as the creator of the rule, have the ability and permission to change any rules that are no longer working for you.

If a rule is making you feel miserable, I humbly suggest you consider changing that rule. If it is not working for you, have your Inner Teen create a new rule for your Inner 7 Year Old to follow. I promise your Inner 7 Year Old will be compliant and follow *if your Divine Wise Self says it is okay*. Set yourself up to Win.

I know you may think this is cheating, but who created that rule?!!

Another game is to identify all your negative self-talk. Get to know your "Should Monster." This is the one that will shoulda-woulda-coulda you to death if you let it. Let your Should Monster know he or she is not real and she can go back to monster-land, or the closet.

What are you doing to make yourself bad-and-wrong, or to make yourself feel unsafe?

(By this point, you can see that 99% of the work is getting the mom back in her power, back in her safety zone.) The way to get back in your power is to give yourself permission to feel good about yourself right now, in this moment, without any stipulations. You can give this to yourself or you can withhold. It is in your power to choose. I'm guessing by this point you know the consequences of each.

If you're feeling like you're needing a voice, feeling like you aren't being heard or that you're not getting your turn...if you're feeling like your boundaries or limits are being pushed, or if you're in that righteously indignant feeling of having been pushed too far, or you're feeling like your life is without purpose, that something is missing, or that you're not living your passion, then you're most likely experiencing the identity crisis of the Inner Teen.

Ask your Inner Teen these questions:

Who am I mad at? What am I sick of? What am I mad about? What's missing? What's next? What would you like to say that you're not giving yourself permission to say? What would I like to do that I cannot or have not done to this point? What would I like to have more of in my life?

Then, of course, give yourself permission to write or journal every outrageous, unthinkable, blasphemous thought you have. There is a difference between writing it down and acting it out. There is a difference between allowing yourself to think it or feel it and saying it to someone else. If you don't give yourself permission to express these thoughts at least to yourself or with someone you can trust and know it is just your Inner Teen venting and not the story you want to create and live yourself into, then you will take these thoughts or frustrations out on your kids, and you will subsequently see this unexpressed issue, whatever it is, in your child.

When I'm stuck in an Inner Teen rant, I either journal and find the mirror within myself, or if I'm really stuck in it and can't even think to journal, I call a safe friend that I have prepped ahead of time to not believe a word of my story and stay at the 30,000-foot level until I can find my wise self to love up my young self that is in pain.

Sometimes at the beginning of the call, I tell them I am really deep into my story, please don't believe anything I'm about to say, and help me utilize the 10 Keys to transform these big, huge feelings that are enveloping my joy, compassion for myself, and playfulness.

Usually in the conversation, in a very compassionate way, my friend will help me find the humor in my serious, stuck, wrong-making, blaming, young self. I will be given permission and encouraged to playfully turn up the volume to an even more exaggerated state, until I'm good and ready or sick and tired of being sick and tired of my current emotional state. Sometimes this lasts longer than I'd like to admit.

You can also use this process when you are looking at others when *they* are stuck in it!!

If you're seeing the three-year-old in your child, then they're not feeling safe, either.

If you're seeing the seven-year-old in your child, then they are feeling like they can't get it right, either. They feel like they're bad-and-wrong, too.

If you're seeing the teen in your child, then they have something to say, too. That Inner Teen can show up withdrawn, sullen (*I don't care*) or irrational and blaming, judgmental and critical. What's underneath those outward feelings? That's what it feels like is happening to them.

So, once we've identified our primary issue with mom, what to do?

If mom needs acknowledgement, then do a Brag List. If mom needs to vent, ask yourself the questions that allows you to vent.

Then when the mom's ready, I help the parent look underneath the child's behavior. So if the child is having sibling rivalry and being just an absolute jerk to his younger brother, I ask, "what could be going on that could cause him to be that way?"

We then, essentially, repeat the above process with the child.

You ask your child if he is hungry, angry, tired, lonely, scared, hurt, or overstimulated. What is going on in the environment that might be causing your child to be acting out? Is there something going on at home—if you and your partner are fighting, sometimes your child might be acting out in order to pull your focus and become the problem, rescue you, in a way?

At school, is the child having difficulty with math, or are they being bullied, or are they having sexually stimulating thoughts that are making them uncomfortable?

This detective work, this question-and-answer process, is how you put the 10 Keys into action.

10 Keys Examples

My son's classmate just attempted suicide. He seemed like a normal kid, no drugs, no behavioral issues, so this came as a total shock to his family. And my son seems very blasé' about it, which makes me sick with worry. How can I know if the same thoughts are going around in my son's head?
– E.L., Dublin, California

Every day in this country, hundreds of kids attempt to take their own lives, and parents rarely see it coming. So no matter how casual your child seems to be, you need to sit down with him and ask direct questions: "Have you ever thought about killing yourself? Why would you do it? If you had a bad day and felt like suicide, what would keep you from doing it?"

That last question is a big one. If your son can't tell you why he wouldn't take his own life, he needs counseling. So don't settle for the first casual answer. Drill down and get a genuine response. And have the conversation often, especially if other family members or friends have attempted suicide. It can be seen as an option that other children may not even consider.

10 Keys Roadmap

The primary keys I evaluated as I answered E.L.'s question were:

Compassion Have compassion for yourself as a mom—in other words, the boy's death is most likely going to scare you or freak you out, which would be normal.

Affect The son is not feeling feelings, or is not feeling safe to express feelings, around someone's death.

Own Your Story Try to think of what story that child might have had in order to go to that extreme, and ask your son questions, *"What was he thinking about the world, about his life? And what are the stories you have about yourself?"*

❉

My daughter brags about getting drunk at a party or making out with a guy on her IMs or MySpace. When I confront her, she says people just say such stuff so that others will think they are cool. Do I believe what she says or what she writes? – J.S., Walnut Creek

When your daughter says she's writing these things so other people will believe it, tell her, "Well, honey, it worked—I believe you're doing these things. So park it right there and let's talk." Then talk through the issues. If she's fabricating these incidents, you may find out in the course of the conversation. And if she's not, you're taking the first step in dealing with it. You may never know for sure; it really does not matter. What matters is what she wrote and you deal with it as if it were true. If it is not true, next time, she will be less likely to take credit for something that could get her into such hot water or "processing conversations."

You might also remind her that if her friends believe what she's writing, so will everyone who ever reads it: other boys, family members, teachers, future employers and college admissions officers, among others reading her profile that she no longer owns. Anything that goes up on MySpace or any other Internet property is like a giant online billboard that can stay there forever. There's no such thing as a permanent eraser on the Internet. So whatever she writes could follow her for years to come. I've heard of many stories of people losing important opportunities because of some innocent post. This is an excellent time to talk about consequences of all posting and the fact that you do not legally own what you write in these environments. Specifically, Facebook and MySpace own all content posted through their sites.

10 Keys Roadmap

The primary keys I evaluated as I answered J.S.'s question were:

kNOw Your Boundaries	Whatever you say, people will believe, whether it's the truth or not. So you're either lying or you did what you said you did, so either the child has broken a boundary about lying, or about actually doing the things she wrote about.

kNOw Your Boundaries	If you deal with the situation as though the girl actually did these things, she will learn a consequence that people believe what you say and lying has costly consequences. This will be helpful in keeping her word and building future Self-Trust.
Own Your Story	When the girl wrote those words, she was manifesting and living into those words. You can ask her, "*Is this the world you want to live into? What is the consequence of living this story? Would you like to create a new story for the future? What would be the consequence of that new story?*"
Intrinsic-Extrinsic	Whatever's intrinsically going on, you are extrinsically manifesting. Whatever the feeling was that made the girl feel like she had to lie, that need is still unfulfilled. As a mom, if the child is acting out for attention like this, she most likely needs help creating a peer group for herself. You can help her get involved with a singing group, a chess club, or whatever the child is most interested in. You may need to help her Organize her Support Village.

My daughter is being pressured by her friends to drink, break curfew, and become sexually active. She tells me she doesn't want to, but thinks she'll have no friends if she doesn't. How can I protect her from peer pressure?

First, it's great that your daughter trusts you enough to come to you with this problem. Having a communicative relationship like this is half the battle. That said, however, this is one of the toughest challenges a teen faces, because status with friends is everything in this developmental stage.

Let your daughter know that much of what she's hearing from her friends is probably baloney: many teens aren't as adventurous as they pretend to be. You can support your daughter by having rules, curfews, and other boundaries that keep her safe, which is what she wants, and by stepping up to play the "bad guy" role with her friends. You can even corroborate with her to have a plan that she gets to blame you for not going along with what they want. Until she has the power and confidence to stand in her own power, let her borrow yours. And finally, you might ask her how she would feel about widening her circle of activities, such as adding a job, sports, clubs, or community work, that might take her away from her old friends and introduce her to some new ones.

However, if this problem truly proves too large for her to handle, you may have to step in and take her away from her friends by changing her school setting. As traumatic as that can be for a teen, it's better than the consequences she could face as a result of giving in to peer pressure: pregnancy, STDs, substance abuse, or an arrest record.

10 Keys Roadmap

The primary keys I evaluated as I answered the question above were:

Own Your Story	When the girl felt she needed to comply with the other teens' demands, she was creating a world and living into their words. You can ask her, *"Is this the world you want to live into?"*

Playful-Messy	With Playful-Messy, you play with the idea of making a mess of your life. So you'd ask the child, *"How far do you want to go with this?"* and playfully explore the life or lifestyle suggested by those peers.
kNOw Your Boundaries	You can ask your child some questions: *"Are you willing to be raped in order to be popular with these people? Are you willing to die in order to be popular with these people? Are you willing to go to jail in order to be popular with these people?"* If the child's answer to these questions is "yes," then it's time to get help. If she answers, *"Of course not, that is a stupid question!"* then ask her what her boundary line is.

This is not that you need to know or that is for her to tell you the answer, but for her to think about it and know this answer for herself.

Intrinsic-Extrinsic	The girl does not have an inner sense of self, an inner sense of worthiness. She is not feeling good about herself. One of the reasons children are so responsive to peer pressure is that they don't know what they want and they need (because, as we've seen, the child is living for the parent and not herself).

The work this girl needs to do is to figure out what she wants, what she needs, and how to have self-care so she will have a sense of value and worth. When you have a sense of value and worth, then you don't focus on the things outside of you.

❁

One of my daughter's school friends has lost a shocking amount of weight. My daughter says she's doing cocaine and everyone knows about it—except her parents. Should I call the parents and tell them? I barely know them, and I don't know if they'd be grateful or resentful for not minding my own business. – M.G., Danville

By all means, tell them. Wouldn't you be grateful if someone did the same for you? The girl's life may be at stake, and her future certainly is. Every parent would want to know, **even if they react defensively in the moment**. The downside to telling them is that you're uncomfortable butting in. The downside of *not* telling them could be a destroyed young life. It's no contest. **Care enough to take the risk and tell them**. Quickly.

There is one potential exception: if you feel the parents will react negatively and further endanger the child, then you can call Child Protective Services, whose legal mandate is to do what's best for the child, advocate for the child, even if that action or outcome would be at odds with what the parent might want.

The reason most parents even hesitate is to protect their own child from being a snitch or to avoid creating drama in their child's life. This is another time that by helping your child understand that there is no contest when it comes to not caring enough to save another child's life in order to save their reputation or avoid drama. What would they want another child to do for them if they were in danger of going to jail or dying? Would they want another parent and child to choose to save their life? The answer also goes back to the previous answer about helping the child have enough inner resources and self-esteem that not telling does not even become an option.

When we feel good about ourselves, we naturally and normally want to serve and protect others. When we feel bad about ourselves, we are in fear, lack, scarcity, and worry about what others might think about us and our own consequences.

10 Keys Roadmap

The primary keys I evaluated as I answered M.G.'s question above were:

Mirror, Mirror If you put yourself in that situation, what would you want as a mom?

Self-Trust Trust your intuition: the reason you're asking the question is because you know you need to talk to the other parents. The reason you're afraid to is because you want to avoid drama and conflict.

kNOw Your Boundaries One of your boundaries may be to do what it takes to protect children, for example. For example, if you knew a child was being sexually abused, would you talk about it? If so, what's so different about a child doing cocaine—because a child is in danger there, as well. And finally, what are you teaching your child by *not* speaking to the other parents?

My youngest daughter has started referring to herself as a loser, but she is really smart and gets straight A's. She says the other kids call her a loser and a geek. She's not—she's lovely and has a few nice friends—but I'm afraid she will stop doing well in school in order to fit in with the other kids.
– J.A., Hayward

This is a big problem, and a pretty common one. Nothing is more important to teens than fitting in, and it is not unusual at all for top students to let themselves slide back into the crowd. Concentrate on building your daughter's self-confidence so she can handle the teasing for what it is, which is jealousy of her accomplishments. Child actors, teen models, and even some top athletes experience the same thing. So work to convince your daughter that the teasing is because of her success. And watch her grades extra-closely for any signs of slippage. See if you can find groups and opportunities where she can be around fun and challenging academic situations.

10 Keys Roadmap

The primary keys I evaluated as I answered J.A.'s question above were:

Own Your Story	When the girl felt she needed to comply with the other teens' pressures, she was creating a world and living into their words. You can ask her, *"Is this the world you want to live into?"*
kNOw Your Boundaries	You can ask your child some questions: *"Are you willing to be raped in order to be popular with these people? Are you willing to die in order to be popular with these people? Are you willing to go to jail in order to be popular with these people?"* If the child's answer is "yes," then it's time to get help.
Intrinsic-Extrinsic	The girl does not have an inner sense of self, an inner sense of worthiness. She is not feeling good about herself. One of the reasons children are so responsive to peer pressure is that they don't know what they want and they need (because, as we've seen, the child is living for the parent and not herself).
	The work this girl needs to do is to figure out what she wants, what she needs, and how to have self-care so she will have a sense of value

and worth. When you have a sense of value and worth, then you don't focus on the things outside of you.

Organize Your Village If your child is out of place due to her intelligence over that of her peers, you can help her organize her village, put a group around her, that is more like her. This way, the child's social needs are more likely to be met, and there is much less chance she will dumb herself down in order to fit in based on peer pressures.

While doing laundry, I found condoms in my daughter's jeans pocket. Should I be glad that she is responsible or worried about her having sex at 16? D.B., Benicia

You probably feel a lot of both, and that's understandable. Whatever you feel is appropriate. The real question is how you should handle the situation. The standard parental impulse is to confront her and tell her what to do, based on what you believe is right...but what reaction is that likely to produce? In my experience, that tends to push kids away. It's more productive to keep the conversation non-confrontational. That keeps you two connected and makes her feel safe in talking to you about what's happening, which is a good thing, because leaving that condom in her pocket where you could find it was no accident. Consciously or unconsciously, she wants to talk to you about it.

So your first line should be, "Honey, I found this in your jeans. Let's talk about it." Then ask lots of questions about how she feels and what she knows about the emotional risks of sexual activity. But don't interrogate her. Your goal is to keep her talking.

If she stops talking, it is because she does not feel safe. See if there is anything in you that is judging, condemning, or controlling her situation. See if you can make peace with that from within and then let her know you cleared it, 'fess up to what you found, and try again. Let her know it is your intention not to judge, condemn, or control her, but to trust and help her trust herself to do whatever will make her life the conscious manifestation of her ideal dreams and outcomes.

Not only know your boundaries, but know your boundaries as a mom. Have a plan how to keep your child safe; give them the tools to stay safe.

Help your child know her boundaries. One way to do this is to role-play with her. Play out several different examples and help the child work through it. It helps to be aware that many children may feel they need their mom to be the bad guy.

For example, if you were at a party and a guy your age, (older, younger, one you liked a lot, one who was most popular, one you feared, friend of the family, etc.) tried to get you to have sex—kissed you, touched you and you wanted to, touched you and you didn't want to, touched you and you had never thought about it and were not sure if you would regret it or not—*What would you do? What would you need from me and how could I help? What could a code word be or text so I could get you out of there without you feeling threatened to speak your truth?*

You can also say: You may or may not want to answer this question out loud to me, but might want to write this down and journal it.

More questions that may help the dialogue between you: *What would it be like after-the-fact if it turned out you did not like the guy and had to look at him the next six years of school? What would it be like if you really like the guy with all your heart and you later found out he slept with one of your friends—are you ready to handle that pain?*

You might even have your daughter or son help you come up with the different examples for you to talk about. Keeping the lines of communication open is the key for both of your sense of safety and to help your child protect herself.

For single-parent women with sons or single-parent men with daughters, it can really be helpful to have a trusted family friend of the same gender for the child to talk to, and be able to offer this to the child as a supplement or alternative to talking to the parent.

Because this conversation can be embarrassing or difficult, here is an example of how to open conversation and some of the questions that might follow.

> *Part of life and love is to love hard while at the same time keeping yourself safe.*
>
> *How can you put more conversation around the entire emotional aspect of love? Are you able to be whole and complete, not expecting someone else to complete you?*
>
> *Are you ready to have adult pain? Are you ready to have adult responsibilities?*
>
> *Are you ready to have adult consequences? If the answer is no, then you're not ready to have sexual relations.*
>
> *If you're asking yourself "am I ready," then most likely you're not quite ready for whatever you're considering. What might be missing?*
>
> *If you see something on the Internet that you're confused about, or that you've never seen before, my intention is that you will always feel comfortable to talk to me about it.*
>
> *The Internet is a tremendous tool for research and democracy. However, like any tool, it can be dangerous if not used safely.*

I am always open and available.

Be ready to answer those questions for your children. If you're not ready to have that conversation, then your kids won't come to you.

You can only say "you can talk to me about anything" when you are ready to handle anything and have the inner resources to mean it. If you can't work this process, get some help so that you can be there fully, in your compassionate, loving power, for your child.

10 Keys Roadmap

The primary keys I evaluated as I answered D.B.'s question above were:

kNOw Your Boundaries	This is one of the questions where it is really important to know their boundaries. *What is your ideal relationship? What relationship issues are non-negotiable for the child? If you get pregnant, are you ready to make the hard decision of what you would do with that baby?* In addition, what is your boundary as a mom? Are you ready to raise another child (your grandchild)? If you don't know, or don't have this boundary as a mom, then your child also does not have this boundary.
Affect	Affect is getting you present to all of the feelings, good and bad, that may be coming up. With Affect, you try to be present to all the feelings of joy, of love, but also of fear and jealousy, which may very well happen.

Own Your Story

In some cases, if the mom got pregnant as a teen, there is a conscious or unconscious desire to live into that story. The child may want to be just like you—after all, things worked out for the mom, didn't they? If the mom is determined that the child not make the same mistake as she did, if the mom is really attached to a different outcome, then the child might, through defiance, live herself into repeating the mother's pattern.

❈

We are wondering about our daughter's sexuality. We have a pretty open relationship with our 16-year-old daughter. She has had a boyfriend for awhile and I know things are progressing. I have talked to her a lot about the big step and waiting and the pressure that boys might put a girl under. She claims there is no pressure, that she wants it, as well, that she has sexual needs. Are girls today really so much freer with their sexuality than we were as kids? – W.C., Martinez

Scientists tell us that young people today mature physically, and sexually, at an earlier age than they did a couple of generations ago. Many parents I work with tell me they had premarital sex back then, but it just wasn't much of a topic of conversation. One reason kids may start earlier today is that parents are busier, so they provide less supervision for their teens. And unsupervised teens will explore sexually.

Your effective communication with your daughter is crucial here. Instead of telling her what you think she should know, you can help her explore her feelings, particularly about the emotional consequences of early sex. Ask her how she will feel if her sexual involvement becomes public knowledge, or if her boyfriend has sex with someone else, or if she gets pregnant or infected with an STD, which in some circumstances may last a lifetime or even shorten a lifetime. And let her know that if she regrets her decision later, you'll be there to support her. If you can't slow her down with your questions, you can at least help her prepare for such a huge step.

Your control, Mom, is limited. You certainly don't have to allow a rendezvous in her bedroom or pay for a hotel room, but if she wants to do this, she will. At least with the reservoir of mutual trust you've established, the lines of communication will stay open.

They may be physically freer, but emotionally are not.

10 Keys Roadmap

The primary keys I evaluated as I answered W.C.'s question above were:

Self-Trust Trust your intuition: the reason you're asking this question is because you know you need to talk to the other parents. The reason you're afraid to is because you want to avoid drama.

kNOw Your Boundaries This is one of the questions where it is really important to know their boundaries. *What is your ideal relationship? What relationship issues are non-negotiable for the child? If you get pregnant, are you ready to make the hard decision of what you would do with that baby?*

In addition, what is your boundary as a mom? Are you ready to raise another child (your grandchild)? If you don't know, or don't have this boundary as a mom, then your child also does not have this boundary.

So what if my room's a mess, clothes everywhere?
It's my room and I should have the freedom to do
what I want. Why can't my parents get off my
back about this neatness thing? A.A., Benicia

Isn't it a bummer to have your own space and have it belong to somebody else? It's your room, but it's their house, and they don't see the boundaries the way you do. So I'd suggest sitting down with your parents and getting clear on those boundaries. If you're leaving old food in the carpet and the place is rank, that's one thing, but if you're just dropping clothes on the floor, maybe just keeping the door closed would be sufficient. Get clear on what's okay with them and what isn't, and negotiate some compromises. You may find them more willing to respect your space if they're confident you're not actually doing anything that could drive down their property values or cause a stench through the rest of the house.

This won't be the last time this issue comes up, by the way. You'll be having the same argument later with your college roommate and your spouse. So use this as practice.

10 Keys Roadmap

Note that this answer applies to children of all ages, not just teenagers. The child who refuses to put toys away is similar in this regard to the teenager with the messy room. The primary keys I evaluated as I answered A.A.'s question above were:

kNOw Your Boundaries	You get to set boundaries on what belongs to you. So when you're ready to buy your own car, house, or rent your own space, then you get more freedom to say what you will or will not do. (Even in a rental or some homeowner associations, you still do not control the world, even if you own it. Sometimes we answer to codes, legal limits, neighbors, etc.)

When you're ready to truly be accountable, you will earn the freedom to make a lot of decisions, but you'll also incur the cost and consequences.

So even though it's a drag for people to tell you what to do and when to do it, it's their right to do that when it's their property. And it is your right to be frustrated, upset, and I might even suggest determined to make your own money, so you will have the opportunity to have your power.

What I would tell the parents is that if you have too many rigid rules, your child will snap. They may say "I'm outta here" and leave before you're ready for them to leave, and more importantly, before they're developmentally ready to leave. Also, if your rules have no room to bend, then they may find other ways to defy you behind your back.

You might reach a compromise that the child can have his room any way he likes, but he must keep the door closed at all times so that the mess doesn't affect anyone else in the family. The more you can find ways to compromise, the more peaceful your environment will be.

Playful Messy

Sometimes kids may need to experience Playful-Messy, especially if they've lived with perfection, or in an environment with a lot of rules. They may need to experience what it is like to live the mess.

There may be consequences, of course...if the child wants to have a friend over, you might be too embarrassed for anyone outside the family to see your home that way.

Mirror, Mirror

To the parent, is there any mirror going on within you? Go look at your desk, at your car...is there anything going on that is reflected? If that's not it, then take a look at your internal world, and see if the internal representation is congruent with the external world, either for you or your child.

If the child's behavior in this situation gets on your last nerve, the likelihood is that there is some issue to be discovered or revealed within you.

Self-Trust

Trust your intuition: the reason you're asking this question is because there is some part of you that actually knows the answer. The reasons you are even asking are because you doubt you have the right to set a boundary, or maybe you are worried you're being too rigid. Look within and listen to what's behind your question.

✻

How can I get my 3-year-old son to stop lying? He lies right to my face about everything from getting his homework and school projects done to who he's talking to on the phone.

Let's face it, children lie (so do adults), even when they're sure to get caught. Every parent seems to have a cute story about their child denying that they've eaten something, even though it's smeared all over that angelic face. But it stops being cute when it impacts the relationship between the parent and the child.

Finally, I recommend evaluating your own behavior. Are you totally truthful with your spouse, your boss, your friends? Do you share every thought, every impulse? If the answer is no, then expecting your children to live to a higher standard is a recipe for conflict, and potentially, pain. It helps to remember that lying is a natural, normal developmental stage.

Do you promote a culture of honesty in your house? Do little white social lies tend to fly? And can your child tell the truth without being punished for it? If the truth is going to cause negative consequences, your son is more likely to lie.

I would suggest two courses of action. The first would be to make sure that it's in your son's best interest to tell you the truth, which means not punishing him for honesty, even if you don't like what you hear. If he admits not doing his homework, you don't take away privileges: you have him do it before you move to the next activity.

The second course of action is more direct. He can't lie if you don't ask, so skip the questioning and find out the answer for yourself. If you want to know if his homework is done, walk into his room and check it. If you want to know who he's talking to on the phone, pick up the extension. When your son is outraged by these invasions of his privacy, your calm response is, "Sorry, son, but you forfeited your privacy privileges when you lied to me. My job is to keep you safe at all costs. When I am once again convinced I can trust your word, you can have your privacy back. The best way to get me out of your business is to be honest with me." And assure him repeatedly that he will never be punished for telling you the truth.

10 Keys Roadmap

The primary keys I evaluated as I answered the question above were:

Self-Trust	Teach your child about self-trust and that you are your word. As you lie, you no longer trust yourself, as it's really hard to remember all of your lies; they cause you stress and pain.
	What you tell others is what determines whether you'll be believed or trusted in the future. If you lie about something and are caught, you won't be trusted next time.
Intrinsic-Extrinsic	Whatever I'm lying about, I'm living myself into.
kNOw Your Boundaries	To the child: do you want to be a person of your word and be respected? Then you have to keep your word and respect others.
	To the parent: try to be compassionate to the child. Understand that they are most likely lying to keep from being wrong, being in trouble, and their actions are not personal.

I knew what to do when my child was a baby and a toddler, but I don't know what to do with my pre-teen. What's our role now? He just tells me to bug off.

Isn't it too bad there's no owner's manual for this? There's really no one universal response to this question, but generally speaking, this is the time when your job transitions from telling and teaching the child what to do into more of a coaching and supporting role, with a whole lot of asking thrown in.

Your biggest responsibility now is to set clear boundaries that your child can operate within, and making the hard decisions that keep him safe. And the best thing you can do to help him begin the transition into adulthood is to ask questions that may help him make his own decisions. "What would you do if somebody at a party offered you drugs? What will you do if your ride home is drunk?" The idea is to get him thinking about the consequences of his decisions. That will gently establish a baseline he can use to make wiser choices. But not all his decisions will be wise ones, so let him know you'll be there for him if he messes up—and fasten your seat belt. And, by all means, never bug off. He is just talking big. He needs you now more than ever.

10 Keys Roadmap

The primary keys I evaluated as I answered the question above were:

Compassion	Fall in love with yourself for how it feels to have your little baby-angel tell you to go away.
	That's their way of trying to grow up and get strong and ready to go, before you kick them out of the house.
	No matter what your child says, you do whatever you need to do to keep them safe and stay connected to them.
Organize Your Village	Make sure your children have other, suitable mentors and peers in their lives, so as your children grow away from you, they will have access to people you respect and trust.

Self-Trust   Put yourself in your son's shoes. Is his "bug off" meant to tell you he needs some privacy? Or is it his way of telling you not to do his homework for him, or that despite what he's been saying, he really *does* want you to come see him get his varsity letter award?

❁

How do you deal with raging teens? My 17-year-old son's anger seems to get out of control sometimes. Is this a normal part of the process or does he need counseling?

Perhaps both are true. Raging emotions are certainly common to children of all ages, and emotional control is something that has to be learned. Whether your son needs counseling depends on whether you can handle and accept his anger and help him understand it, and whether he's endangering either you or himself with his rages. If these outbursts include any kind of threats or actual violence, then safety becomes the primary issue, and it's time to call in professional help. Trust your instincts. If anything he says or does scares you, get help and support for your Inner 3 Year Old so she can feel safe, as well.

10 Keys Roadmap

The primary keys I evaluated as I answered the question above were:

Affect   This concept bears repeating, so I will say it again: emotional control is something that has to be learned. Until then, ideally, your child will feel safe enough to feel his feelings, especially with you.

Mirror, Mirror

Is your child reflecting how you're feeling within, or how you'd *like* to feel within, but are not allowing yourself to feel? Is your child experiencing someone else's rage, possibly when you're not around?

Or, as another example, is another family member undermining your power? I've seen many times how a grandparent becomes the authority over the mother. What happens when you visit your folks?

One mom told me how, when she and her family visit her mother, the kids will pop in to ask her a question, and then stop themselves and say "Wait—why am I even asking *you*?" At grandma's house, even the children realize that mom isn't the authority.

In general, when you don't find your power with your own mom, you're setting up a pattern to repeat itself with you and your children.

One of the costs of patterns like these is that the pattern continues...unless your child is the one to be brave enough to break it.

kNOw Your Boundaries

Your child is trying to answer these questions:

What is an appropriate way for me to express my feelings? How can I express my rage? What is okay?

Is it okay to yell? Is it okay to hit my bed? Is it okay to journal and write anything I want to write and my mom or dad will not read it? Is it okay to express my feelings to your face? (Or will I have to express those feelings behind your back?)

Set three absolute boundaries with your children, to help them until that time when they are able to set these boundaries for themselves:

- you're not to hurt yourself physically
- you're not to hurt anyone else physically
- you're not to destroy property

Beyond that, I invite parents, challenge them to consider, that the more boundaries you have, the less you are able to express them fully.

Let me close this section with the ultimate example. What happens when your child drops the ultimate bombshell: *I hate you!*

With your 10 Keys, compassionate self in charge, how might you answer?

Try this:

Okay, I can see you're upset and you are letting me know in the meanest-maddest-baddest way possible. I get it. You are really mad. And you can say those things to me, and I'll be fine, but I just want to share with you that if you say these things to anyone else, you're likely to get a different response. 'I hate you' is a really powerful expression, and you might get some really intense reactions and negative consequences from others.

This acknowledges the child (*Affect*), helps them understand the boundaries, that it's not generally okay to speak that way to just anyone (*kNOw Your Boundaries*), and simultaneously keeps the dialogue open so you can keep talking to your child, and your child can keep talking to you.

Conclusion

I hope you find this book refreshing and new, and at the same time, like you've found your old best friend, like you knew all of this but had just forgotten it.

If you listen to yourself, know that you have the answers, and so do your children.

Reconnect with your inner, intuitive divine wise self, who knows you better than anyone does, or ever will know you, and your job is to help your child connect with his or her inner, intuitive divine wise self—your child has that same inner resource in herself.

If the 10 Keys still seem uncomfortable, or if you're finding yourself unsure how to apply them, or you have more questions, please feel free to connect with the a 10 Keys support group, where you can get the compassion, education, and emotional follow-up support you might need.

What if all the children of parents who read this book could live into these new words...

Exercise: Connect with Your Inner Family

1. What do you think you need most for each member of Your Inner Family? Everything that is in the Inner Family Chart is a possible answer.

3 year old	Feeling of Safety

What will meet that need? What if there was nothing to fear? What if I was safe in my skin, no matter what?

To really challenge your thinking, read Victor Frankle's *Man's Search for Meaning*. He found a way to feel safe in a concentration camp, being tortured, having his family killed, etc. His message is: you can impact me physically, but you can never own my mind. He says, "We cannot avoid suffering but we can choose how to cope with it, find meaning in it, and move forward with renewed purpose."

7 year old	Feeling of Accomplishment

How do I get to win? What makes me feel successful? I get to change the rules if I can't win.

If you don't like your life, look at the rules you have created (dishes must be done before you go to bed—who made up that rule? Is it still working for you? Children must go to bed by 8:35. Who made that rule? Is it working for you?)

Teen

Feeling Passionate about life and your life's purpose and full, authentic self-expression.

What if you were at least able to think the unthinkable, the blasphemous? What if you listened to that rowdy, bodacious, outrageous thought? You don't have to act on it, but your thoughts might inspire you to stand up for your rights, consider the possibility of saying no to one more trip to the mall, to giving and giving and giving.

What if setting your boundaries was actually a gift to those around you? What if saying yes when you really want to say no was a lie, giving when you are exhausted actually caused another to feel like they are too much for you to handle and that they are killing you off, so in turn, they no longer stay connected to their needs and don't even know what they think! This is what happens when it becomes too dangerous to have feelings and needs because the parent cannot protect herself from her child.

2. Describe the "Ideal" family for each member of Your Inner Family.

3 year old   You could create an inner mother and father for your emotional self to give your young self all that you could ever want or need.

How about an ice cream bar of thousands of flavors, how about a purple swimming pool with floaties, slides, and parents holding and moving you through the relaxing, revitalizing waters. How about a room full of your favorite toys, how about anything your young self might possibly imagine—and multiply the gifts times a thousand. The sky is the limit.

What would fill up your Grand Canyon of emotional needs? Is it words, physical touch, gifts, people, places, or things? If you can think it, you can have it. Your mind does not know the difference between a visualized picture-image or actual reality.

7 year old   You could create an inner mother and father who told you everything you had ever wanted to hear, who believed in you despite all odds, who saw your greatness despite the evidence of the past. These inner parents told you that you were complete, worthy, accomplished, successful, and could now choose to do only what you want to do, that which will bring you joy.

Teen   You could create an inner mother and father that could hold your rage, your jealousy, your entitlement, your blasphemous thoughts and desires. You could give yourself your own fan club, your own cheerleading squad, your own inner football team, an entire business team to accomplish your wildest passions and desires.

For example, my Inner Teen has an entire auditorium with a huge fan club. The bottom tier is filled with screaming teens stepping into their power and ready to live into their greatness, the middle section of the auditorium is filled with powerful, awakened, inspired, alive parents loving life and loving the greatness of their child's passionate leadership and authentic voice.

The top tier is filled with people who support Teens and Parents of teens—youth directors, teachers, support professionals, coaches, healers, therapists, etc. This group is totally filled-up from within and has an abundance of overflow to support and compassionately understand the parents' and the teens' challenges.

Wise Self	An Inner Wise Ideal loving mother and father self for every age.
	These wise beings are duplicated for every young need and there to heal every traumatic experience I have ever thought I experienced during my entire life. After giving this Wise Self to every age and re-living, healing, transforming every scary, hurtful, "negative" experience of my life, my Wise Self helps me to glean the golden nuggets and gifts from every traumatic life experience. I'm given the opportunity to relive it, transform it, and give my young self a new story and support system for every experience that I thought made me all alone and ruined for life.

3. Describe the "Ideal" child for each member of Your Inner Family.

3 year old	My Inner 3 year old is given the permission to become present to every feeling I might not have even known I felt at the time. My Inner 3 Year Old gets to experience and become aware of a vast range of emotions and experience safety and bliss at all possible extremes, from ecstasy to rage, to sadness, to fears, etc. My ideal inner child is aware of physical sensations, emotional sensations.

7 year old	My Inner 7 Year Old feels complete and accomplished. She no longer has the rules that make her want to chase the proverbial moving carrot. She is now living by new rules that set the entire Inner Family up to win, to experience bliss no matter what may come. My Inner 7 Year Old feels safe with my 3-year-old having irrational, illogical emotions and the Inner Teen dreaming, conspiring to live into the impossible dream. My Inner 7 Year Old chooses to do tasks for the joy of creating, acting, moving life forward, experiencing whatever may be.
Teen	My Inner Teen is living into her authentic life passions, no matter how unrealistic others may think those are. She is connected to her emotional 3-year-old and feels like a protective, loving big sister. She is proud and appreciative to her hard working 7-year-old inner sibling and appreciates the thoughtful, critical, challenging questions, yet stands firm in her beliefs and is willing to take risks, knowing there is no real way to ever fail. She knows that real failure is hiding under the covers, staying in the stands, silencing her voice, and never trying to do and live into her life passions.
Wise Self	My Inner Wise self is all-knowing, all-compassionate, all-giving, all-loving, omnipotent, omnipresent to all the inner emotional states. She is the holder of bliss and limitless possibilities.

4. Describe the "Ideal" parent for each member of Your Inner Family?

3 year old	An Ideal Parent for my Inner 3 year old is strong, intuitive, compassionate, loving, and has an infinite capacity to hold any and all feelings for limitless amounts of time. My ideal mother and father self each have the patience of a saint and the insight of spiritual divinity.
7 year old	An Ideal Parent for my Inner 7 Year Old tells me over and over and over and over and over again that I am once and for all good enough. My ideal mother and father selves see and name thousands of gifts, talents, accolades, awards, and accomplishments.
Teen	An Ideal Parent for my Inner Teen is a parent who can handle, hold, encourage, and not be destroyed by my rage, my blasphemous thoughts, my sacrilegious beliefs, my sexually provocative desires, my irrational/illogical visions and dreams. My ideal mother and father selves encourage me to express, feel, experience, live, play full-out, and continually ask the question HOW GOOD CAN YOU STAND IT?
Wise Self	An Ideal Parent for my Wise Self is a parent who helps me find, see, identify, hear, and meet my highest Inner Wise Self. The Ideal Parent and the Wise Self may be seen as one and the same

Wise
Self

being, or the Ideal parent may be more of an imagined Ideal human being, while the Wise self is the connection to your soul's spiritual self.

Acknowledgements

In writing this book, I was assisted by several wonderful people:

Let me begin by expressing my appreciation to Dora Wallace, my business and life partner, and truth be told, designer of this book. I am grateful for her embodiment of what it means to be an adult Teen. She provided me a wealth of intellectual, emotional, physical, and spiritual support, as well as the direct experience of what Teenology is all about.

I am grateful to the many friends who helped to keep me grounded during the past few years and offered encouragement at some of the most opportune times. There are too many to mention individually. But, I offer special appreciation to Athena, Marci, Lori, Naomi, Alicia, Barb and Jennifer, each of whom has pushed me to challenge myself, empathized with my troubles, and encouraged me with their own struggles and words of wisdom.

I also want to thank Rie Langdon, my developmental editor, the challenging voice for all mothers, and the patience of a saint to capture all my ADD moments. Thank you also to Alicia Dunams, my book coach and book parent behind the scenes. She was going to help me give birth to this book one way or another. And we DID IT!!! Thank you so much, Alicia Dunams, for believing in me and helping me see this through.

I would affectionately like to thank my beautiful mother for her years of unwavering support, her psychological expertise, and her unconditional love that modeled the endless possibilities that has made me who I am today. I am grateful for my father, who has been a most prominent figure in my life, for his encouragement, grounding words of wisdom, and unfailing belief in me and continual support. Without the love and support of my family; Dora, my mother, my father, my brother, and my two teen experts, Zach and Jackson, this book would never have come to fruition.

Hopefully, all of you see that the love and care that I have put into this book is the extension of the love and care that you have shown me. Thank you for your love, compassion, and playfulness in helping me make this dream a reality.

Dr. Beth Halbert is a licensed child, family, teen psychologist who has a 25+ year history of working as a dynamic facilitator, speaker, and management consultant. Beth has a thriving private clinical practice and facilitates national workshops for parents and teens. Her keynote presentations for organizations are known to be both highly entertaining and extremely educational. Her clinical focus has been in the area of secure attachment through healthy emotional development.

Dr. Halbert received a BA in Psychology from Baylor University, a MEd in Human Resource Development from Vanderbilt University, and a PsyD in Clinical Psychology from the California Institute of Integral Studies. As a psychologist, coach, educator, speaker and songwriter, Dr. Beth brings warmth, passion, and playfulness to her work.

She was an outside trainer and consultant for Saturn Corporation's initial Training and Development team, Chrysler's Customer One Phases I–III Initiative, and Cadillac's Nationally Awarded Standards for Excellence program. Dr. Halbert has also worked with JD Powers, McGraw-Hill, Honda, Toyota, and Volkswagen as a facilitator, keynote presenter, coach and consultant, offering compelling ideas on how to improve communication between leadership and employees, how to create new avenues for motivation, shift any fear into a challenge that can be easily broken down and handled, set optimal focused objectives that you will reach with everyone having fun in the process and end repetitive patterns of things that no longer work.

As a licensed child psychologist and leading expert in parenting teenagers, 'Dr. Beth' has worked with hundreds of families to create stronger parent-teen bonds. As the moderator for Dr. Beth's Compassionate Parenting National Teleconference Series, she takes a unique approach to helping both teens and parents overcome the difficulties of adolescence, combining proven clinical practices with warmth, playfulness, self-expression, and compassion. Dr. Beth knows how teens think and act. She understands how to get them talking about their emotions and behaviors. Plus, she knows parents. She understands how to get them to accept themselves exactly as they are, and how to accept their children exactly as *they* are. She assists parents and teens in building positive dialogue and developing more connected relationships.

CPSIA information can be obtained at www.ICGtesting.com
Printed in the USA
BVOW030503120911

270806BV00003B/2/P